When God
Steps In

Stories of Everyday Grace

When God Steps In

Stories of Everyday Grace

BONNIE BRUNO

Standard®
PUBLISHING
Bringing The Word to Life
Cincinnati, Ohio

Published by Standard Publishing, Cincinnati, Ohio
www.standardpub.com

Text and photos copyright © 2007 by Bonnie Bruno

Printed in: USA
Project editor: Laura Derico
Cover and interior design: Robin Black, Blackbird Creative, LLC
Cover and interior photography: Bonnie Bruno

Published in association with the Books & Such Literary Agency,
52 Mission Circle, Suite 122, PMB 170, Santa Rosa, CA 95409-5370,
www.booksandsuch.biz.

ISBN 978-0-7847-2066-0

Library of Congress Cataloging-in-Publication Data
Bruno, Bonnie.
  When God steps in : stories of everyday grace / Bonnie Bruno.
      p. cm.
  Includes bibliographical references.
  ISBN 978-0-7847-2066-0 (perfect bound)
  1. Christian life--Anecdotes. 2. Grace (Theology) I. Title.

BV4517.B67 2007
242--dc22   2007010864

13 12 11 10 09 08 07   9 8 7 6 5 4 3 2 1

This book is dedicated in loving memory

to my parents, ROY AND BETTY JETER,

whose faith and perseverance left a godly imprint

on my life. Someday we'll meet again.

Contents

Introduction

Who can understand the wonders of creation? God spoke, and the world in all its splendor sprang into being. He breathed, and humanity took its position on the first page of history. He stepped in to fill a vast emptiness with his light.

This maker of the universe is still in the business of creating. He knits babies together in their mothers' wombs, infusing each child with a unique purpose. Like that great flaming pillar that led the Israelites in the wilderness, he still keeps watch on the road ahead, directing us along paths that will help, not harm us.

You and I are here because God saved a spot for us at this very moment in history. When life pulls the emotional rug out from under us, as it did when my dad passed away during the writing of this book, God is there to pick us up, dust us off, and speak hope into our weary hearts. When life hands us an award for a job well done, he is the proud Father in the front row. And if we should choose the wrong path and attempt to hide our hearts from him, he lingers and reminds us that we are priceless.

I wonder . . . if we could somehow recognize the many ways God steps into our daily lives, would it change our outlook and attitudes? the way we treat others? how we view our place in the world?

God stepped into my life in a tangible way when I was two years old. My family and I were on vacation, and one evening we found ourselves driving a long stretch of lonely highway. The nearest town was still miles up the road, and we hadn't passed a single vehicle in over twenty miles. My mother had fallen asleep in the front passenger seat, and on either side of me slumped a sleeping brother. While my dad drove, I reached for Mama's purse, and within minutes I had nibbled my way through the contents of her prescription thyroid medication.

Mama awoke and immediately noticed her missing purse. One glance at my pale face told her all she needed to know. Horrified, she screamed for my dad to pull over, and as the story goes, my six-foot-three daddy lifted me out of the car and prayed for God to send someone quickly—anyone!

God stepped into that desperate moment and sent a lone car, driven by a doctor who was heading to a hospital in the next town. We reached the ER in record time and this man rushed me past the check-in desk into a room where he administered lifesaving treatment.

Weeks later, because my parents hadn't received a bill from the doctor or the hospital, they phoned to ask why. Nobody at the hospital knew the doctor by name. No one had seen him since that frantic night. And nobody ever sent a bill. Coincidence? I don't think so. God had stepped in with a sacred embrace and a helping hand. And that's why I'm here today.

Human nature seems to gravitate toward "miracle" tales. We marvel at such happenings much the same way an enthusiastic crowd cheers a fireworks display. Yet, how often are we blinded to God's intervention in ordinary everyday events? Blame it on busyness, self-absorption, or farsightedness; when we miss those moments, we rob God of the opportunity to bless us.

May you sense his sacred embrace as you read how the God of the universe stepped into these fifty lives to leave a lasting impression.

—BONNIE BRUNO

ONE

The Voice of Change

One individual life may be of priceless value to God's purposes, and yours may be that life.

—OSWALD CHAMBERS

Cinde has been singing for as long as she can remember. Star of her kindergarten graduation, she wowed family and friends with a song. In third grade she performed the lead role in her class play, singing "Raindrops Keep Falling on My Head," and at church she never lacked an opportunity to sing before a doting congregation.

Cinde believed her singing voice was a precious gift from God, but she didn't realize that it had become her main source of self-worth. She felt most valued and proud of herself after a public performance.

"I'm always amazed by what God will do to capture a person's attention," says Cinde. "For me, it took a year of silence."

For the better part of 1999, this woman with the beautiful voice could barely speak above a whisper. Trips to specialists confirmed that a collection of nodules was crowding her vocal chords. Removing them posed a serious threat to her ability to sing.

The news jarred Cinde's world. "Why would God do this to me, especially after I'd recently recommitted my singing voice to him, to use however and wherever he saw fit? I had given him my voice and now he was taking it away. It didn't make sense."

Looking back, she now sees the bigger picture. God needed to perform a work in her heart. To complete it, he would need her full attention.

During the season of silence, Cinde was forced to take a deeper look at her life. Her past was dotted with one disappointment after another, yet she'd learned to mask her pain and put up a front that didn't match her inner turmoil. "Until then, I didn't understand that those past experiences were preventing me from moving forward in my walk with God," she explains.

To outsiders, Cinde appeared carefree and happy, but God knew the truth: she had built a barrier around her heart and was using it as a dumping ground for unforgiveness, bitterness, and resentment. The Lord used those silent months to open her eyes to the real Cinde—the person he loved and understood through and through.

She recalls a moment that would alter the course of her life: "Suddenly I realized that I needed more than just my voice healed. I began to ask God to help me forgive those who had hurt me, and to tear down my protective wall."

To outsiders, Cinde appeared carefree and happy, but God knew the truth: she had built a barrier around her heart and was using it as a dumping ground for unforgiveness, bitterness, and resentment.

God responded by wrapping his arms around Cinde in a way she had never experienced before. "As his love surrounded me, a deep healing took place within. All the hurt, rejection, and fear came crashing down. He set me free!"

God planted a special seed in her heart and soul—one that Cinde prays will continue to bear fruit for him long after she has departed this world. As the seed sprouted and grew, she noticed a change in the way she approached people and situations. God helped her recognize people who were dealing with the same destructive emotions she had secretly harbored for years. She could hear anger and pain in a child's voice, bitterness in the reaction of an unappreciated store clerk, and signs of rage in a frustrated husband. What's more, God filled her with a compassion that enabled her to reach out to each wounded person.

> ALTHOUGH IT'S EASY TO SEE WHEN SOMEONE HAS A BROKEN ARM, CINDE KNOWS FIRSTHAND THAT IT IS MUCH MORE DIFFICULT TO RECOGNIZE A PERSON'S INNER PAIN.

As the months wore on, her family and friends joined in prayer for Cinde's full recovery. She visited a third specialist at Vanderbilt Voice Clinic and underwent several months of vocal and singing therapy. "It was a process that took many months of obedience and faith," says Cinde. "As I worked with the therapists and allowed God to touch my heart, my voice grew increasingly stronger. He not only restored my voice, he handed it back to me better than before!"

God's plan for Cinde didn't end there. Now in full-time ministry as an associate evangelist, she travels to various churches, where she shares her personal story in word and song. Always, her message points to God's faithfulness at every level of our lives. Although it's easy to see when someone has a broken arm, Cinde knows firsthand that it is much more difficult to recognize a person's inner pain. For that reason, many of the songs she writes and sings deal with the topic of healing and restoration.

"The voice of change is never easy, quick, or painless," says Cinde. "That journey often involves the road less traveled, simply because wounded people have a tendency to anticipate more rejection and hurt."

The woman with the restored voice now assures her audiences, "Listen and you will hear God's voice—calling out your name. He wants to reach down and pull you out from under the heartaches that have held you captive for so long. He wants to set you free!"

Finding Reggie

*The Lord does not look at the things man looks at. Man looks at
the outward appearance, but the Lord looks at the heart.*

—1 SAMUEL 16:7

Eileen's work as an alternative high school teacher has
helped her to become desensitized toward the way
teens dress. She has seen her share of outlandish fashion
and makeup—goth, geek, grunge, jock, prep—but one
day Reggie showed up to change her perspective forever.

He arrived that first day wearing dark, heavy, eye
makeup, and he'd gone to great lengths to paint his
long, pointy fingernails in varying shades of green and
black. "Reggie portrayed a creepy, devilish grin better
than any actor," remembers Eileen.

Starving for attention, this teen proved to be her greatest challenge. He regularly turned in obscene papers, and would add to class discussions by making shocking statements that repulsed or insulted fellow classmates. His actions seemed aimed at creating the greatest shock effect.

Eileen found herself in a frustrating dilemma, on one hand counseling colleagues as to the best way to reach him, yet feeling repelled by his appearance and attitude. She'd been trained to work with challenging students, but the more time she spent with Reggie, the less she liked him. "Rarely do I dislike students, but my feelings for Reggie were heading south in a hurry," she admits.

During a quiet moment at home, Eileen ran across a familiar Bible verse that challenged her to treat others the same way she wanted to be treated. God used those words to enable her to look deeper, past Reggie's appearance and bizarre behavior.

"Having grown up in an abusive home, I recognized his cry for help the instant I met him," she says. She knew that in order to help him, she would need to make a change in the way she viewed him. "I needed to see Reggie as God sees me—as a beautiful person who is loved in spite of imperfections."

Eileen prayed for God to equip her for the challenge ahead and to fill her with a love that would spill over into the way she approached this troubled student.

Although it wouldn't be easy, she believed that God is able to work in and through the toughest situations.

Before the school day began, Eileen sat in her classroom and mentally rehearsed the verse she'd read earlier that morning. As the morning wore on, she found it easier to overlook Reggie's gaudy makeup and disgusting comments. She focused on ignoring the old Reggie and, with God's help, tried her best to view him through new eyes. "I began to see him as I wished teachers in my past had seen me—as a tortured soul needing attention."

> I BEGAN TO SEE HIM AS I WISHED TEACHERS IN MY PAST HAD SEEN ME— AS A TORTURED SOUL NEEDING ATTENTION.

In the days and weeks ahead, Eileen prayed for God to supply creative ways to interact with Reggie. God answered by simply blinding her to everything external. She engaged Reggie in conversation whenever possible, but didn't respond to his outrageous, attention-seeking statements. She focused on smiling more, nodding her head to let him know she was listening, and kept their exchanges as positive as possible.

Eileen says she'll always remember the day Reggie bounded into the classroom, dropping his book bag at his seat. He headed straight for her desk, waving a book he'd been reading, then shared how the book had challenged him to think of himself in a different light.

Surprise spread across Eileen's face as she read the title aloud: *Wild at Heart*, by John Eldredge. The men at Eileen's church had used it in a small study group recently and had raved about its message.

When the school bell rang, Reggie headed for his desk, but couldn't sit still. He returned to hers and asked, "You know how you always ask us to write for the Teen Page? Well, I want to write about something. I'll write it now and you can look at it. See what you think. Is that OK?"

> REGGIE'S WORDS FILLED HER HEART WITH AWE.

Eileen nodded, then turned her attention to others in class. Before the end of the period, Reggie kept his word and delivered a handful of papers. His writing described a journey of hatred toward himself and others, adding that he partially accepted the "concept of God."

Then came the kicker: "God shows up in weird places—even English classrooms. My teacher lets me say outrageous things and then asks soul-searching questions. Questions that lead me to think more about God."

Reggie's words filled her heart with awe. *God truly does show up in weird places and in weird people like Reggie and me,* she thought.

Now every time a new student shows up in her classroom, she remembers her experience with Reggie. "I try to look at what really matters—each person's heart."

THREE

That's Life!

Those who are disciples of the Lord Jesus
should labor with all their might in the work of God as if
everything depended upon their own endeavors.

—GEORGE MUELLER

Rick grew up with a dad who loved working with his hands, but according to Rick, "Not everything he worked on needed fixing, and not everything he fixed worked right ever again." Rick's tree house and sandbox were situated close to the garage workshop, so his dad often recruited him to help.

"One day he hollered to me from his spot underneath the car, to tap the pistons on an engine he was overhauling." Eager to help, Rick left the sand castle he was building and scrambled up on top of the engine. "How was I to know sand and pistons don't mix?"

Rick stepped in to help his father whenever he could. Smashed thumbs, lopsided buildings, and "windows painted shut so tight, dynamite couldn't have opened them" were frequently the order of the day. He never was able to convince his dad that the black paint he spilled on a freshly shingled porch roof was a good thing. (Rick thought it added a "dairy-cow ambiance" to their farmhouse.)

When he was six, Rick received a set of tools from his dad, "mostly so I would stop losing his. I was so proud of my cotton nail-pouch, Stanley tape measure, and wood-handled hammer, I began work immediately on a rabbit hutch." Within minutes he'd smashed his thumb and lost his new tape measure.

Nothing was off limits when it came to his father's version of home improvement. Rick remembers one such project, when his father plumbed all the faucets backwards, so the hot water was on the right and the cold water on the left. "Although Dad died before I built my first home, I found myself wishing that we could have worked together on its construction," says Rick. To honor his dad's memory, Rick plumbed one of the new shower faucets backwards.

ONE DAY WHILE READING HIS BIBLE, RICK CAME ACROSS A PASSAGE THAT WOULD CHANGE HIS DAILY FOCUS.

One day while reading his Bible, Rick came across a passage that would change his daily focus. "I was astonished to read in John 5 that Jesus delighted in working with his Father." Verse 17 reads, "Jesus said to them, 'My Father is always at his work to this very day, and I, too, am working.'"

That single passage helped Rick understand that instead of simply joining God in whatever work he had for him to do (as he used to do with his own father), he had been struggling to follow a long list of self-imposed rules. Yes, he believed wholeheartedly in God's saving grace, but says, "The day-to-day grind of walking out my faith seemed to consist of more don'ts than dos."

> I'VE FOUND EXCITEMENT IN BOTH THE ROUTINE AND THE UNCOMMON.

He had wrestled with everyday issues such as not getting angry in traffic, steering clear of gossip, and trying to be encouraging instead of critical. He worked at ridding his mind of impure thoughts and refused to splice the truth, but his resolve usually melted by noon. "I spent the majority of my evening prayer time apologizing," he says.

Since those days, Rick has discovered a newfound joy in serving God. "I've found excitement in both the routine and the uncommon." He sees that God wants to convey his love both to him and through his life. "If love is the ultimate litmus test of a believer's faith, then sharing that love—the Great Commission—involves asking God for instructions."

Now, no matter where life takes him, Rick believes his

heavenly Father has work for him to do. "I once discovered God at work in Nicaragua, when a filthy street urchin begged me to hold her," he says. So moved was he by that starving child, he resigned from pastoring a church whose members were enmeshed in a heated issue centered around replacing the pulpit furniture. He made the decision to join God in ministering to the poorest of the poor.

Rick's eyes and ears are alert to God's detours. He says he discovered the Lord at work one day when he missed his flight and had to drive twenty-four hours to reach home. Later he realized that the inconvenience was well spent; God had used that time to speak to his undistracted heart.

Since fine-tuning his relationship with God, Rick discovers glimpses of the Lord even in daily interruptions that used to annoy him. He has learned to watch for what he calls "that moment in the mess when God's love can invade." He has experienced the difference between working *for* God and working *with* God. When he works *for* God, he burns out quickly by an addiction to activity; but when he chooses to work *with* God, alongside his Father, he feels infused with energy and purpose.

Rick admits to still smashing his thumb occasionally. He's known to lose a tape measure now and then too. "But I get to work with my Father—and that's life!"

FOUR

A Different Answer

*The best and most beautiful things in the world
cannot be seen or even touched—they must be felt with the heart.*

—HELEN KELLER

At three days old, Tim and Carrie's second child, Macey, was diagnosed with a rare medical condition called Aicardi Syndrome. Carrie recalls, "Although I cannot remember the face of the doctor who delivered the news, I will never forget his words."

He must have come to the wrong room, thought Carrie. He couldn't be describing their child, using terms like *severe disabilities*, *daily seizures*, *blindness*, and then this jarring statement: "Most children do not live to see adulthood." How could God allow such a thing?

In the beginning, Carrie says, there were days when it was difficult to even get out of bed in the morning. "I remember watching healthy children Macey's age who were smiling, babbling, and learning to sit and crawl. Sometimes all I could think about were the things that she would never be able to see or do." Once while watching a beautiful sunset, Carrie realized that her child would never have that opportunity. "It was heartbreaking to think that she would never see our faces or smile back at us either. I wondered how the world could continue turning, when the depth of our pain was so great."

For the first several months, Carrie says she prayed every day for God to take away the seizures. She begged him to change Macey—to cure her from this condition that limited so much in her life. But it was not to be.

"God didn't answer my prayers for a miracle—our daughter was not healed. But he did answer my prayers for a change," says Carrie, "and the change happened within us. He changed our hearts and helped us to recognize what a blessing he had given us."

> HE CHANGED OUR HEARTS AND HELPED US TO RECOGNIZE WHAT A BLESSING HE HAD GIVEN US.

Many well-intentioned people have passed through their lives with words of advice that did little to encourage them. One cliché they heard often was, "God will never give you more than you can handle." Carrie didn't find that always to be true. "Sometimes God did give us more than we could handle, but in those moments he also reached out and allowed our hearts to grow in ways that we never could have imagined. He helped us to accept what seemed at first overwhelming."

Each month and year with Macey has brought new changes. Sometimes they're big changes, like the tracheotomy she underwent last year. Other changes are less serious, yet require another adjustment. "We've learned to accept each new piece of the puzzle that comes with having this very special child. I always say that Macey has taught us more in life than we could ever teach her. We've learned not to sweat the small stuff, to cherish the happy moments and always look for the positive, and to realize that life is precious. None of us is guaranteed a certain amount of days."

Macey has never spoken a word, yet she conveys an incredible sense of peace and unconditional love to everyone who spends time with her. "Her happiness is contagious and her smile can melt a heart," says Carrie. She has transformed the entire family, as well as given them a heart for people with disabilities. "We recognize the struggles and joys of those who live each day with special challenges. It's an understanding that most people can't possibly realize unless they've faced something similar in their own lives."

Macey has also taught her older sister, Caleigh, lessons in compassion. "Caleigh has a way of looking past people's differences. Her teacher recently told us that she always seems to seek out children who don't fit in or who are having a hard time at school. She looks for ways to include them in activities at recess. We know that having Macey as a sister has changed the way Caleigh approaches her world."

Although they still experience occasional hard days, they're now able to find joy in "almost every situation. Every now and then, I glance at a child about Macey's age," says Carrie, "and I imagine what life would be like if she were healthy and able to run around." She quickly adds, "But I'd never want to return to those early days of sadness and despair. I know that God sent her into our lives for a reason, and we feel blessed to have been chosen as her parents."

Macey is exactly the way God created her to be. "We thank him for every day he gives us together and pray there will be many more to come."

FIVE

Just a Little Lie?

If we confess our sins, he is faithful and just and will
forgive us our sins and purify us from all unrighteousness.

—1 JOHN 1:9

Du ring her first twenty years of life, Jeanelle's parents, grandmother, and aunts served as stellar role models. Their honest examples and faith in God were pillars, offering her a strong, secure home base. "But I didn't realize how deeply they'd influenced me until the period after I left home."

Jeanelle attended a Christian college, and as many new college students learn, the lessons that would stick with her for the rest of her life would begin that first year. Unfortunately, she also discovered that she would soon learn her best and most unforgettable lessons by making mistakes.

"More than anything else, I longed to become the woman God intended for me to become," says Jeanelle. After college she dreamed of following a path that would both honor God and make her family proud of her. That longing was stretched and strained many times over, beginning with her marriage to a minister of education at a large Dallas, Texas church.

Jeanelle quickly grew attached to a group of women who became her main circle of support. "In my role as a pastor's wife, I often found myself in the center of an uncomfortable spotlight. It was an extremely demanding role for any young woman, but God graciously provided friends who won my admiration and respect."

> MORE THAN ANYTHING ELSE, I LONGED TO BECOME THE WOMAN GOD INTENDED FOR ME TO BECOME.

One day a close friend, Vicki, shared a piece of news with Jeanelle in confidence, making her promise that she would not breathe a word to anyone. "Of course I won't," Jeanelle assured her. And in her heart, she truly meant it.

Shortly after their meeting though, Jeanelle ran into Rita. Rita, Jeanelle, and Vicki were a tight threesome, so it seemed only natural to let Rita in on the news. After all, what were prayer partners for? In her heart of hearts, she knew that she ought to keep quiet, but her compassion and concern won out. Like a witness on the sidelines, she heard herself repeating everything that Vicki had told her in confidence, word for word.

Sickened and horrified by what she'd done, Jeanelle agonized over the fact that it was probably too late to repair the damage. What if Vicki were to find out that she'd betrayed her trust? What if the whole church were to hear about it? How would they view their pastor's wife from that point on?

Her worst fears came true. It didn't take long for the truth to surface, and one day Vicki tearfully confronted her. Was what she had heard true? Had her good friend really broken a confidence?

Jeanelle flew into a major panic. Faced with the awful truth, she reacted by dramatically declaring, "Oh no, Vicki! I would never do that!"

> JEANELLE FELT LIKE SHE WAS THE ONLY PERSON ON EARTH WHO HAD EVER BROKEN HER WORD.

Her spirit and self-esteem sank to a new low. Not only had she run her "motor mouth," but on top of that offense, she'd tried to cover her deceptive tracks with an ugly lie. "I felt physically ill, shamed to the core. How could I have backed myself into a corner like that?"

In her despair, she cried out to God. "What have I done? What's wrong with me? How will I ever be able to repair the damage?"

Jeanelle felt like she was the only person on earth who had ever broken her word. She couldn't eat, couldn't sleep, and had convinced herself that no other wife of any minister had ever caused so much havoc. How could she have betrayed a dear, trusting friend like Vicki?

"In my heart, I knew that there was only one way through my dilemma," says Jeanelle. "I'd have to confess—and soon." She worked up the courage to approach Vicki.

> GOD TRANSFORMED THE MEETING OF TWO FRIENDS INTO A SWEET MOMENT OF CLEANSING.

It's a moment she'll always remember. "In true fatherly fashion, God had other plans in mind. He transformed the meeting of two friends into a sweet moment of cleansing—not just for me, but for both of us. We hugged. We cried. And Vicki not only extended grace and forgiveness, she also shared something she says she'd learned from my attempt to right a wrong—the true meaning of humility and forgiveness."

"I've been needing that example in my own life, Jeanelle," Vicki told her. "Thank you."

Jeanelle gained something priceless that would forever change her impulsive ways: a crash course in tongue-taming. "Now I always pause and think twice whenever I'm tempted to share a confidence or relay a half-truth," she says. "My experience taught me about the bitterness of a lie, how it feels to break a confidence with a close friend, and how traumatic it is to have to face that friend with the truth later."

Above all, God uses the memory of Jeanelle's humiliating brush with deception as he continues to mold her into a woman after his own heart.

Beauty from Ashes

I will turn their mourning into gladness;
I will give them comfort and joy instead of sorrow.

—JEREMIAH 31:13

Most little girls dream of fairy-tale romances, storybook weddings, and happily-ever-after lives. LeAnne was no exception. From a very young age, she believed that she was destined to meet that special someone. At age twenty-four, she fell for a man who seemed like her ideal prince and committed her love and life to him in marriage. Together they claimed Robert Browning's famous verse as their motto: "Grow old along with me! The best is yet to be." The future held great promise, or so LeAnne believed.

Ten years later, though, her husband experienced a change of heart. He shared news that would rock her world: not only had he fallen out of love with her, he also had decided that he no longer believed in God. In early 2002, he filed for divorce.

Seemingly overnight, LeAnne's storybook life was reduced to ruins, only a pile of ashes left to show where her palace had been. She remembers the day in great detail. How could this happen to her—to them? She loved her husband so much. How could he turn his back on her and Madeline, their young daughter?

LeAnne was also concerned about her husband's sudden change of heart toward God. Where would life take him, now that he had made the decision to turn his back on the Lord? Endless questions swirled inside her head daily—questions for which she had no answers.

Facing each day became a huge effort. LeAnne says there were times when she probably would have stayed in bed, if not for Madeline and two hungry dogs. Even worse were the long nights. "In the shadow of nightfall, grief, fear, and loneliness were my constant companions."

Many nights found her lying facedown in her closet, weeping and praying. She'd never experienced such deep grief, and began to understand the Old Testament tradition of covering oneself with ashes. After her tears were spent, God's peace flooded her heart in a way she hadn't experienced before. "My Father was with me.

He loved me and would not leave me. My hope rested in him alone."

As the days wore on, LeAnne prayed that her pain would not be wasted, that God would somehow turn her heartbreak into new growth. He answered her heart's cry by drawing her close and equipping her to become the person he had created her to be. He revived her passion for writing and speaking; and through those gifts, she is now able to encourage and comfort others.

> AS THE DAYS WORE ON, LEANNE PRAYED THAT HER PAIN WOULD NOT BE WASTED, THAT GOD WOULD SOMEHOW TURN HER HEARTBREAK INTO NEW GROWTH.

"My daughter loves kinder-garten, reading, and coloring," LeAnne says proudly. "She's learning to pray, and I know God hears her prayers just as he hears mine."

Three years after her heartbreak, God surprised her with a new prince—one who loves LeAnne and her daughter and, most importantly, loves the Lord with all his heart. "When it was time to tell five-year-old Madeline that Mart and I were planning to marry, I took her to breakfast one Sunday morning before church. Over waffles and eggs, she and I talked and played and colored."

LeAnne wasn't sure how her daughter would respond. How would she react to the news that their twosome was about to become a threesome? With a deep breath and a silent prayer, LeAnne began. "Madeline, you know how much I care about Mart, don't you? And you know how much he cares about me?"

Madeline nodded.

"We love each other. He has asked me to marry him, and I said yes."

Madeline's blue eyes widened. Her mouth formed a big O as she processed the news. Then, to her mother's delight, she danced in her seat and sang, "My mama's getting married! My mama's getting married!"

> THE LITTLE GIRL WHO ONCE DREAMED ABOUT A FAIRY-TALE LIFE IS NOW OLDER AND WISER.

Everyone in the restaurant stopped eating and stared. LeAnne burst out laughing at Madeline's joyful response. She reached across the table to hug her precious daughter and tearfully thanked God for smoothing the way.

LeAnne knows that the little girl who once dreamed about a fairy-tale life is now older and wiser. God took her pain and disappointment and turned them into a priceless lesson about his character and provision. Through hardship, LeAnne has learned that her true bridegroom is really the Lord, now and forever, who lovingly transformed the ashes of her life into a thing of lasting beauty.

Asking for Apples

*Beware in your prayers, above everything else, of limiting God,
not only by unbelief, but by fancying that you know what he can do.*

—ANDREW MURRAY

A few years ago, Gail's husband lost his lucrative job in the computer field due to an unexpected downsizing within the industry. Prayer became her family's everyday staple as they faced great financial stress.

Though the job would pay much less than what they'd been used to, a security firm valued her husband's experience as a former law enforcement officer and hired him to work the night shift. During that time, Gail discovered the challenges of trying to keep a busy five-year-old and an inquisitive three-year-old quiet while Daddy slept during the day. On many days, she just wanted to forget all her problems, but God showed his faithfulness by helping her think creatively about the challenges her family faced. He even inspired her to come up with new ways to save money when it came to meal planning.

One morning, Gail wanted to fix her children's favorite breakfast of chopped apples, nuts, raisins, and sunflower seeds. To her disappointment, she discovered that they had run out of apples. All she could find was one pathetic little withered apple sitting on an otherwise bare refrigerator shelf. She peeled it anyway and cut it into portions as usual. "My son, who loves apples, eyed the fruit suspiciously," Gail remembers. "He said, 'Mommy, is this the only apple we have? It looks tired!'"

His question cut deep, and his honesty filled Gail with a strange mixture of laughter and sorrow. "The apple is fine, son," she assured him, "but it's all right if you don't want to eat it. Mommy will go to the store later and buy us some new apples."

He left his pile of apple chunks in the middle of his plate and scurried off to play. His sister picked at her portion of the apple too, and left hers for the trash. Witnessing the kids' disappointment served as a reminder of their bleak financial crisis.

Gail found her purse and dug through its contents, hoping to find enough change to buy fruit. "I could barely believe that I had to dig for change in order to buy something as simple as apples, but this was our reality," she says.

As the day progressed, Gail worked on various writing projects to avoid going to the store. By mid-afternoon, frustration caught up with her, and she couldn't concentrate on her work. Hot tears streamed down her cheeks as she wondered what lay ahead.

> BY MID-AFTERNOON, FRUSTRATION CAUGHT UP WITH HER, AND SHE COULDN'T CONCENTRATE ON HER WORK.

"My husband was doing the best that he could, so perhaps our situation was really my fault," recalls Gail. She thought about taking on a job outside the home. "Questions hammered me with nails of frustration. Who would care for my children? What hours could I work? Would I make enough money to matter after we paid for child care?"

Gail did the only thing she knew to do. She cried out to God for direction. "Lord, I know that you can do anything, but I need something specific from you today. It doesn't matter what it is. It can be something as small as my finding enough money to go to the store for some big, juicy, red apples. Father, I just need you to show me that you love me."

Gail recalls a wave of comfort washing over her. She went about her busy day in anticipation of God's answer.

A couple of hours later, a UPS truck pulled up in front of her home. The driver didn't ring the doorbell.

"We hadn't ordered anything, but he left a box at our door anyway," says Gail. She nearly fainted when she pried open the box and peeked inside. There sat thirty-six of the most beautiful red apples she had ever seen!

Gail and her children danced around the kitchen together. "As I served my babies apples, I was awed by the fact that God had done something so wonderful. This encouraged me to ask for more of what I believed that he wanted for me. If he cared enough to bring apples to my doorstep, how much more did he want to do for me?"

That simple box of apples reminded Gail that words are important to God. "He longs to give us our heart's desire. He longs to hold us in his lap and give us the sweet, juicy apples of his love. He wants to cover us with the kisses of his mercy and shower us with the fresh fruit of his grace. He wants us to call on him even for the small things."

She no longer worries about digging for change, because the Lord proved that she was the apple of his eye. "He changed my anguish into laughter with a simple doorstep delivery."

Eight

The Gift of Home

The best is yet to be.

—Robert Browning

Flora could blame her shivering on her car's heater, which had gone out on one of the coldest mornings in January, but she knew that she was trembling from fear too. During a recent visit to her doctor, he'd discovered lumps and labeled them "suspicious." She was heading to the hospital to undergo tests that would determine whether the lumps were malignant or benign.

Bargaining with God was not her usual style, but she found herself praying, "If you'll let me have my life . . ."

God heard and answered. After a stressful period of waiting, test results showed that the lumps were not cancerous. The experience—what she calls her "confrontation with mortality"—did change her life. It made her hungry to learn as much as she could about the hereafter. What was Heaven really like? The Bible spoke of it, yet she yearned to know more.

Then she realized something both simple and profound. Heaven is like coming home! Sir John Bowring once quipped, "A happy family is but an earlier Heaven." Flora had warm memories of growing up with her mother, grandparents, and a maiden aunt in the 1950s. Her memories revolved around a particular home—her grandparents' elegant Victorian home in rural Staten Island, New York.

WITHOUT A FAMILY, THE OLD HOUSE WAS JUST A SHELL.

Flora remembers it well: "With a grand stairway, polished hardwood floors, spacious rooms with beautiful ceilings, and a crackling fireplace, the house seemed like a mansion to me." The house was saved from virtual ruin by her grandfather, who worked to restore it.

Flora revisited the house through her elderly mother's photo album. Unfortunately, the doors to that Victorian mansion closed forever to relatives after her grandparents died. Losing both her beloved grandparents and the home where her childhood flourished was a heavy load to bear. "The sorrow those losses etched into my heart makes me grateful for the promise of a heavenly home—a home beyond the reach of death or time," says Flora.

The loss has given her added insight into God's love for each of us. "Only after my grandparents were departed did I realize how blessed I was to have received such personal attention from my family." Heaven was sounding sweeter all the time, as God pointed out similarities between her earthly home and the heavenly home he promised to all who believe. He also reminded her of the sheer joy of setting aside the worries and disappointments of this life. "I believe we will find in Heaven the fulfillment of lost dreams and desires. We will also find earth's heartaches understood in Heaven's light," says Flora.

One day, she and her mother decided to return to the old family home, which had given birth to such fond memories. "It was disheartening. Abandoned and deteriorating, the house had once again fallen into ruin. Gone were the peaceful woods across the street, replaced by tall buildings that overshadowed my former home."

EARTH'S DEAREST DELIGHTS ARE BUT FLEETING SHADOWS COMPARED TO THE WONDERS GOD IS PREPARING FOR THOSE WHO LOVE HIM.

The two women walked into the once-beautiful yard, now overgrown and littered with trash. They peeked through grimy windows at rooms filled with clutter. God spoke to her heart and opened her eyes to the sad truth: Without a family, the old house was just a shell. The life she remembered there wasn't about the structure or the furnishings; it was about the loved ones who had transformed the house into a home.

"I regret that most of my family members were gone before I met Christ, and I had nothing eternal to offer them." She turned from the windows, and her gaze settled on a solitary purple iris poking out from among thick weeds. It reminded her of a maiden aunt who had listened to Flora's testimony of her newfound faith. When her aunt had accepted Christ for herself, Flora had exclaimed, "I'll see you in Heaven!"

Not long after that, she learned that her aunt had suffered a fatal heart attack. "Today I still see her in those old pictures. And I know we will meet again. She waits with our heavenly family of believers, who will die no more."

As Flora and her mother left the deserted old mansion, she thought of the days when it was home. *If I could reenter those secure, old doors, I would be greeted by the waiting embraces of loved ones,* she thought. *I would be enveloped by the beauty of elegant rooms, warm with firelight and the glow of love. I would also find a place at the dining room table, prepared just for me.*

"So much more awaits the Christian, when Heaven's gates of pearl open to welcome us home," says Flora. "Earth's dearest delights are but fleeting shadows compared to the wonders God is preparing for those who love him."

God could or would wor
quickly, she decided t
a week, she figured
familiar black b

It didn't h

Julie
a

Humble yourselves, therefore, under God's mighty hand,
that he may lift you up in due time.
Cast all your anxiety on him because he cares for you.

—1 PETER 5:6, 7

Julie had been battling depression, due in part to a long history of personal loss. So when her two beloved Old English sheepdogs Emma and Chelsea died, it was more than she could bear. In the past, she'd tried hard to lean on God with her problems, but her inflated sense of pride now stood between herself and God. She was tired of pretending.

"So on that fateful night, I invited God to resume his place at the forefront of my life," says Julie. The next morning, she awoke to find that her nine-month bout with depression had lifted. Still not convinced that

47

such a change in her life that
postpone her celebration. After
she would most likely return to that
hole.

appen.

was a dog lover to the core, so when she ran into
breeder quite by accident, she couldn't resist the
invitation to adopt the last pup of a litter. She fell
instantly in love with the cute little fawn-colored pug.
And because of her recent encounter with God's love
and forgiveness, it didn't take long to think of a name
for the new pup. She would call her Grace.

Shortly after taking Grace home, Julie noticed a
troubling physical characteristic. When she took her to
the vet for immunizations, she mentioned that one of
Grace's shoulders appeared higher than the other. The
vet agreed and scheduled an X-ray. Results pointed to an
extreme case of scoliosis at the top of Grace's spine.

"Not only was there a huge curve just past her neck,"
explains Julie, "but at both ends of the curve, the spinal
column was also twisted." The vet explained that as Grace
grew, her spinal column would either straighten out or it
would continue to twist, leaving her paralyzed from the neck
down. If that happened, she would have to be euthanized.

Stunned by the discovery, Julie headed home to absorb
the news. "I'd sit on the steps of my deck and watch Grace

frolic around in the yard, and my heart would ache for her to be whole and well and happy." To some, Grace was probably only a dog, but to a devoted pet owner like Julie, she was everything. Julie kept a watchful eye on her and asked God to grant her pup the same mercy he had granted to her during her period of depression.

A SHORT WHILE LATER, JULIE'S LIFE TOOK AN UNEXPECTED TURN.

A short while later, Julie's life took an unexpected turn. She noticed swelling in her lower legs whenever she worked evenings at her computer. Concerned that this was more than regular water retention, she consulted her doctor, who sent her for a chest X-ray and echocardiogram. Test results revealed that she had hypertrophic cardiomyopathy. "The left side of my heart was pumping out oxygenated blood at only thirty percent of normal capacity," explains Julie. "At age forty-five, I was experiencing the early stages of congestive heart failure."

Julie's doctor started her on a daily regimen of several medications aimed at strengthening her cardiovascular system. "I'd sit on the steps of my deck watching Grace romp happily around our backyard. One day, God spoke to my heart and assured me that if he could guard the health of a playful pug like Grace, he could surely handle my own health issues." He supplied the strength she needed to release her fears and to place her complete trust in him. "From that moment on, my prayers took off in a whole new direction."

Several months into the medication therapy, Julie's doctor sent her for a follow-up echocardiogram to see whether the medication was working. God filled her with the confidence that no matter how serious the results, he would take care of her.

"The next day, I received a phone call informing me that I was officially out of the woods. I wouldn't need to see the doctor for another six months!"

I NO LONGER HARBOR ANY FEAR OF THINGS THAT ARE OUT OF MY CONTROL.

Julie remembers how she let Grace outside that afternoon and stood there crying tears of gratitude. "God had my life and Grace's firmly in his control. I was convinced that he was rejoicing with me at that moment the way I had rejoiced for Grace a few months earlier."

Julie's huge sense of relief is etched in her memory, and her experience has changed the way she approaches life in general. "I no longer harbor any fear of things that are out of my control."

In fact, Julie was so comforted by her newfound sense of assurance, she decided to prove to God that she was no longer worried about her future.

"I went out and adopted a second dog."

TEN

Equipped for Life

From the fullness of his grace
we have all received one blessing after another.

—JOHN 1:16

At age fifty-six, Roger began a journey of grace. He'd spent almost nineteen years working at a Christian organization when it downsized. In the third—and presumably final—career of his lifetime, he suddenly faced the possibility of unemployment. It had been a long-sought-after job, and he'd gladly returned to school in order to gain the skills he needed.

"But God saw what I couldn't," says Roger. He felt like a flickering candle as he tried to adjust to a quickly changing field. His main assignment had changed, and when his employer asked him to join a different team, he felt obliged to accept. It wasn't easy adjusting to his new responsibilities. In addition to personal and job-related stress, Roger also suffered from hearing problems he couldn't afford to correct. He eventually ended up on probation, struggling to prove to his manager (and to himself) that he was capable of carrying out his responsibilities.

Time is a teacher, and Roger is now able to view the experience differently. "What I failed to recognize was that I was no longer on track with God's will." He knew that the situation would only get worse unless he made a serious change.

In his heart, he knew that God had provided work at that particular company. He'd prayed specifically for it, and so he doubted that God wanted him to search elsewhere for employment. To leave would be to abandon God's call, so he refused to acknowledge his job dissatisfaction. He recalls the day he received jolting news. "When I arrived at work that morning, people were standing around engrossed in a newspaper article predicting downsizing that very day. I knew I would surely be laid off, for I was convinced that I was no longer worthy of being kept."

He e-mailed his fiancée to request immediate prayer. After a brief meeting explaining the day's procedures, his team returned to their desks to stare blankly at their computer screens. Anxiety was the mood of the day.

Roger was the first in his department to receive news of

a layoff. The next two hours he busied himself with exit paperwork and benefits briefings. Prayers, tears, hugs, and humiliating good-byes followed. Later, he packed his personal belongings and, with the help of friends, transferred everything to his car.

"As I drove home, unable to take in the reality of what had just happened, I glanced in the rearview mirror. 'You're unemployed, boy,' I said to myself. 'What are you going to do now?'"

He also asked an even more important question of God: "Is this what you really intended for me?"

> I'VE LEARNED THAT DEPENDING ON GOD'S GRACE DAY BY DAY— EVEN DURING THE HARDEST OF TIMES—IS MORE JOYOUS THAN DELUDING MYSELF INTO BELIEVING THAT LIFE IS UNDER MY CONTROL.

God answered by gifting Roger with an immediate sense of calm. Gone was the unrelenting stress over a job that had grown much too challenging. More clearly than ever before, he recognized exactly what it meant to be held securely in God's loving grip.

"He freed me from what had become personally unworkable, and he'd arranged it that way because I'd refused to deal with the problem on my own." Roger believed that just as surely as God had removed him from the job position, he would also provide all that he needed to begin a new life.

"I prayed more fervently during the subsequent weeks and months than I had in years," Roger recalls. God became so real and personal that Roger was inspired to write a song, which says in part:

> I believe God's working behind the scenes;
> He's helping me in ways I can't see.
> God understands all my problems;
> He knows my best efforts are not enough to solve them.
> I believe God's working behind the scenes;
> He's renewing my faded hopes and dreams.
> He always provides the things he knows I need . . .

After Roger's marriage, his wife's income helped support a simpler lifestyle. He found part-time work in a less stressful field. Day by day, God proved himself faithful. Roger recognized that he had weathered the storm only because of God's grace, yet still wasn't quite sure what God had in store for him.

The answer didn't come all at once. His part-time job ran its course. Then he found another. God inspired him to begin writing faith-based novels in his spare time—a path he hopes to continue. Roger has gleaned a lasting lesson out of his experience. "I've learned that depending on God's grace day by day—even during the hardest of times—is more joyous than deluding myself into believing that life is under my control."

Roger had always known that God's peace can override even the most severe storm in life and that he always leads us safely to shore. "But what I'd failed to learn earlier in life is that God often leads us to a different shore than where we were expecting to land."

Fresh Faith

Let us fix our eyes on Jesus,
the author and perfecter of our faith.

—Hebrews 12:2

Bay was a protective mother bear when it came to her sons. Although the idea of becoming a stay-at-home mom was just a dream, she often prayed that it would come true someday.

When her husband was killed at the age of thirty, life became even more complicated.

One day while working, Bay received a phone call.

The caller's voice sounded rushed and garbled. "Bay, you have to come right away!"

"Hello? Sonya, is that you?"

Sonya was Bay's babysitter. She sobbed into the phone, her thick Mississippi accent slurring her words. "Yes, it's me. Raymond's been hit by a car! Massey Street and Dean Avenue. Hurry!" More sobs—then the phone went dead.

Moments before the call, Bay had kicked off her shoes to seek relief on a muggy spring day. The daily cash report lay spread out across her desk, standard procedure for a late Friday afternoon. But that Friday was different in another way. Not only was she coming to the end of another week, but a major chapter of her life was about to end. It was supposed to be her last day of work. The promise of survivor benefits meant that she was finally free to become a stay-at-home mom.

But the caller's news left her stunned. *Raymond, my eight-year-old son—struck by a car?*

Bay grabbed her shoes and rushed in her stocking feet past a coworker's desk. "My son's been hit by a car!" she called on her way out. "Someone else will have to finish the cash report. I won't be back."

Fear grabbed her heart as she slid into the stifling hot car. *Lord, help me to think clearly,* she prayed silently. *I need your strength and wisdom like never before. I don't know what to do!*

God answered by bringing Sunday's sermon instantly to mind. While maneuvering through heavy traffic, Bay repeated her pastor's statement of faith out loud: "God has gone ahead of me and prepared answers for whatever I'm going to face. I can praise him in the circumstances."

Determined to live out her faith, she began singing praises, all the while reminding herself that he would take care of everything, from her son's injuries right down to the last hospital bill. God brought to mind other times the Lord had answered her prayers, and her pastor's words rang clear and true: "Our ears need to hear truth when our circumstances are beyond our ability to believe that God is in control."

> ALONE IN HER CAR, BAY BEGAN RECITING ALL THE PRAYERS GOD HAD ANSWERED, TURNING THEM OVER ONE BY ONE, REVIEWING EACH AS SHE WOULD A PRECIOUS GEM.

Alone in her car, Bay began reciting all the prayers God had answered, turning them over one by one, reviewing each as she would a precious gem.

Traffic lights stayed green for several intersections, but as Bay neared Massey Street, a knot of traffic slowed her to a crawl. She parked the car and raced up the sidewalk, still in her stocking feet. There in the middle of the intersection sat an ambulance. Police cars had pulled in at various angles to control traffic and onlookers.

Bay pushed through the crowd until she reached a paramedic who was kneeling in front of her son. The first thing she noticed was his shirt, which was streaked with blood.

The ambulance worker nudged her back. "Lady, give us space. We're trying to do our job here."

"I'm his mother!"

His expression softened. "Well, it looks like his front tooth has been knocked out."

He went on to explain that Raymond had crossed in the middle of the street, between parked cars. An unsuspecting driver had rounded a corner the moment he darted out into the street.

The ambulance transported Raymond to the closest dentist to have the tooth reinserted, but the clinic was closed for the weekend. However, as it turned out, the dentist had been momentarily delayed on his way out the door and was still there. He stayed to save Raymond's tooth.

GOD HAD SHOWN
THAT HE INTENDED TO
GROW HER FAITH
ONE INCIDENT AT A TIME.

"This is a permanent tooth, forced out by the root. That's why he has experienced so much bleeding," the dentist explained. "Hopefully he didn't suffer any nerve damage." The dentist's kind words were an encouragement.

As she later reflected back on her afternoon, Bay

recognized God's protective hand over the entire situation. It was as if the Lord had gone ahead of them and made provisions for every need, right down to the last detail.

The most surprising discovery came some time later though. The driver who had struck her son was uninsured, yet Bay never received a single bill!

God had shown that he intended to grow her faith one incident at a time. "Each situation in life calls for a fresh flow of faith," Bay declares. "My relationship with Jesus has to stay alive by walking out faith's basics. He is truly the author and perfecter of my faith."

TWELVE

Notes from Heaven

This is the confidence we have in approaching God:
that if we ask anything according to his will, he hears us.

—1 JOHN 5:14

The discount store reeked of stale, musty stock boxes. Half-opened cartons and spilled contents littered the aisles. *This place looks like my life—a major mess,* thought Jenna. Stepping around strewn clutter, she trudged wearily up and down the aisles.

Hammered by the pressures of college, she had reached a point of mental and emotional exhaustion. Although her future appeared full of possibilities, life as she knew it had become a painful prison. She felt numb, trapped in a corner by an unemotional family and a string of empty, ruined friendships. What's more, she detested how she looked. She hated where she lived. It seemed like nothing satisfied her anymore.

So she'd come to the store with a specific plan in mind: buy sleeping pills and put an end to her unbearable life. Deep down, though, Jenna wondered whether she would be able to go through with her plan. Could she really bring herself to swallow the entire contents of a bottle of pills? Hot tears spilled down her face, and she instinctively reached for a box of tissues on a nearby shelf. When she lifted the box, a dusty scrap of paper floated featherlike to her feet. Its simple, handwritten message read, "God Cares, Saves." How odd that she should pick the one box of tissues that had sat upon that old wrinkled note.

Goose bumps spread across the back of her neck as she read the message again: "God Cares, Saves." Jenna remembers exactly how she felt. "I hadn't thought about God since I was a child, way back in Sunday school. I used to listen to Bible stories about miraculous events, and back then I believed every word without questioning."

I HADN'T THOUGHT ABOUT GOD SINCE I WAS A CHILD, WAY BACK IN SUNDAY SCHOOL.

How had she reached such a different mind-set in just a few years? Now she approached God as a skeptic, questioning his very existence. And in spite of the perfectly timed message from under the tissue box, something inside her tried to explain it away as a coincidence. She thought, *Bible-time miracles happened centuries ago. If God really exists, then why is my life so miserable?*

Jenna's hands shook as she folded up the note, slid it into her jeans pocket, and sarcastically summed it up: *Yeah, right—a note from God magically appeared in this filthy, run-down store. It's nothing but a fluke.*

She decided to buy the box of tissues and was waiting in line when something else caught her attention. A small card with bold blue print lay on the floor near her feet. It read, "God loves you." How could this be? Two messages in one day were a bit much. Jenna glanced around, half expecting to see a burning bush like the one that had appeared to Moses.

A SMALL CARD WITH BOLD BLUE PRINT LAY ON THE FLOOR NEAR HER FEET. IT READ, "GOD LOVES YOU."

"In the privacy of my car, I unfolded the crinkled notes, and read them over and over. I remember slumping against the seat and sobbing for an hour. Had God known my plan to swallow the sleeping pills? What happens to people who take their own lives?"

Confused and alone, her mind raced ahead with questions that demanded immediate answers. If God had wanted her attention, he had certainly gotten it! Jenna's thoughts turned to a Bible her aunt and uncle had given her for high school graduation. She hadn't been too excited about their gift, so she'd been using it to prop up an uneven leg on her bed.

After her experience in the store, Jenna drove home and retrieved the dusty Bible. She flipped its pages hungrily, but the words seemed to run together. She decided to phone a local church for advice. "Where's a good place to begin reading the Bible?" she asked.

JENNA ATTENDED A WORSHIP SERVICE AND LISTENED TO A MESSAGE ABOUT GOD'S ALL-ENCOMPASSING LOVE.

"The book of John," answered the pleasant voice on the other end. "Check the table of contents. It'll guide you to the book of John. May I pray for you?"

The thought of a stranger praying for her was too much. Jenna took the easy way out and hung up.

That evening, she struggled through the books of John, Matthew, Mark, and Luke. It all sounded like ancient fiction. *Maybe it would help to actually visit a church,* she thought.

Jenna attended a worship service and listened to a message about God's all-encompassing love. "Let your light shine before men, so they may see your good deeds and praise your Father in Heaven," the pastor recited.

These words showed her how her aunt and uncle had been beacons of light in her life. Their gift of a Bible had brought her to this moment in time. It had begun a journey that would eventually lead her to a personal relationship with Christ.

Once God changed Jenna's heart, she was able to share his love with numerous family members who later turned their hearts and lives over to Christ as well.

Seventeen years have passed since Jenna entered that run-down retail store in a desperate search for sleeping pills. God knew all along that just a few words—notes from Heaven—would turn her thoughts back to that long-ignored Bible and would ultimately change her life forever.

A Done Deal

Faith never knows where it is being led,
but it loves and knows the One who is leading.

—OSWALD CHAMBERS

Jody has been a diagnosed Type I diabetic since the age of ten, when she learned that her body lacked the ability to produce enough insulin. Insulin is the hormone that unlocks cell doors, allowing glucose to enter. Without glucose, Jody lacked the necessary fuel to energize her body. Diabetes stresses major body organs. Among other serious consequences, it can lead to heart attack, stroke, and loss of vision.

Thirty-two years after the onset of her diabetes, Jody's doctor informed her that she needed a kidney transplant. A search began for a matching donor. While she waited,

Jody underwent peritoneal dialysis via a tube inserted into the lining of her stomach. She scheduled her daily activities around three thirty-minute dialysis sessions, all the while praying for a donor. A wait of that nature can take many months or even years. In some cases, a match is never found.

Numerous churches joined together in prayer for Jody and her potential donor. Jody believes that God knew all along who that person would be, and on January 12, she received the exciting news that not one, but two identical matches had been found! Her younger sister and older brother were perfect candidates for the transplant. At the advice of her doctor, Jody chose her brother Dan. If ever she were to need a second transplant surgery in the future, it made sense to save the younger kidney of her sister for later.

"I was worried about the pain my brother would ultimately face," Jody reveals. A donor generally experiences more pain than the kidney recipient, because his role in the transplant involves the cutting and removal of a key organ. "The doctors had been telling us that we would be in pain—especially Dan—but God in his mercy had another plan."

> THE DOCTORS HAD BEEN TELLING US THAT WE WOULD BE IN PAIN—ESPECIALLY DAN—BUT GOD IN HIS MERCY HAD ANOTHER PLAN.

From the day after the surgery, neither Jody nor her

brother needed any of the pain medication prescribed to them.

Six days after receiving Dan's kidney, Jody went to stay with her sister, who lived near the hospital. Jody was soon well enough to return home, and that night—only one week after her transplant—she surprised friends by showing up at her church's Tuesday night prayer fellowship. She'd been braced for a long recovery of at least a few weeks, but Jody believes a healing doesn't always come the way we expect it will.

"I wanted people to see what I had experienced," she explains. "God was healing me in a miraculous way."

Jody has the admirable habit of taking the long view of life. "When I think about how God formed my brother in my mother's womb, it's awesome to know that he was forming a kidney that would be used to heal me one day."

Waiting for a kidney was a faith-stretching experience, yet to Jody it was nothing new. "The previous challenges I had gone through in life are what brought me to that place of faith. Sometimes it's hard and I don't like the road, but the battles are always worth it. In Christ, it's a done deal."

Since her surgery over eight years ago, Jody has taken more pills than most of us will see in a lifetime. For the first several weeks, she took dozens of pills each day to prevent her body from rejecting the new kidney. Now she is on a maintenance plan of four pills in the morning and one at night. At the time of her surgery, her doctors were anticipating a day, hopefully within the next decade, when a transplant patient may need only a shot every year as an immunosuppressant.

Eight years have passed since Jody's kidney transplant. She's doing well and has had few setbacks. "God is good. I don't just say that because of the amazing healing he has given me. God would still be good if I wasn't doing as well as I am."

Jody is a woman who feels securely wrapped in God's love. She has felt it in good times as well as in the midst of incredible struggles. Ask her about her transplant and she'll soon change the subject. Life isn't about the hurdles, but about what she has learned from them. She realizes that even the faith to believe comes from the Lord. As she walks in step with God, he provides the faith and trust to handle whatever the future may hold.

> LIFE ISN'T ABOUT THE HURDLES, BUT ABOUT WHAT SHE HAS LEARNED FROM THEM.

"I'm truly weak in myself, but God has given me the strength to walk through this life. I need him desperately because I know I can't make it without him. My faith alone isn't worth much," she says, "but the God behind that faith is worth everything to me."

Memories Preserved

If you receive yourself in the fires of sorrow,
God will make you nourishment for other people.

—OSWALD CHAMBERS

Judy knows what it means to love and be loved by a mother who placed the welfare of others above her own. "During the holiday season, no matter how much or how little we had, Mom always made a special fruit and nut basket for neighbors in need. She demonstrated her belief that it is always better to give than to receive."

When her mother's Alzheimer's disease cast its long shadow across their family, Judy began a journal of their last year together. The journal details how she ordered Mom's favorite sandwich from a nearby restaurant—

an ordinary event, yet part of the tapestry of their last visit. Other entries describe how they'd gather to reminisce about more carefree days, and some revisit occasions when Judy's daughter would stay up late with Grandma to watch scary movies.

Another entry recalls how they enjoyed browsing through family photo albums. "Mom would sit for hours admiring pictures we'd taken together as a family each Christmas," says Judy. Their last weekend consisted of some of her mother's favorite foods: fried chicken, fresh butter beans, potato salad, broccoli casserole, and peach cobbler. "It was a wonderful time of sharing our love for one another," recalls Judy. "Our son Tim and his wife, Jennifer, were there, along with their sons Connor and Noah. Jennifer scheduled an appointment to have a professional picture made of Mom with the grandchildren. It turned out to be one of my most favorite photos. I included that picture in my journal as well."

Later that summer, the family planned a reunion and gathered in their mother's honor. Judy remembers how thrilled her mother was to have her children and grandchildren in attendance. Another time, Judy and her husband celebrated her sixtieth birthday along with her sister and mother. They let her mom choose the restaurant, and once again a special memory was created—one that would warm her long after her mother was gone. "My sister surprised me with a cake, ice cream, and a singing candle. This was a very special and blessed birthday," she wrote in the journal.

That fall, they took Mom out to her favorite restaurant, the Dillard House, for dinner. All the leaves had changed into gorgeous shades of orange and red. Thanksgiving soon followed, and Judy and her cousin visited her mom. In the true spirit of the season, she wrote about what it means to be surrounded by a loving family: "Being with Mom during this special season is always the greatest gift a daughter could have."

Journaling had become a way of holding on to precious memories. Little did Judy realize that this would be her mother's last Thanksgiving and Christmas. When that final Christmas rolled around, she wrote: "My sisters joined us in this special Christmas holiday celebration with Mom, eating good food, laughing, opening gifts, and most of all, just being together as we rejoiced in our Savior's birth—Christ in Christmas, Immanuel . . . God with us!"

> LITTLE DID JUDY REALIZE THAT THIS WOULD BE HER MOTHER'S LAST THANKSGIVING AND CHRISTMAS.

Judy recalls how she decided to give the rose-colored journal to her mother. It contained descriptions of activities they'd shared, as well as photos of family get-togethers. "I knelt beside Mom's recliner and read this book of love out loud to her."

Now the journal is back in Judy's possession. Reading

it again has helped her realize how God purposefully stepped into each visit, as if to tap her on the shoulder and say "Remember this always." He is the one who prompted her to begin a journal that would later become a cherished gift for her mother.

"I thank my God for all he continues to do in our lives," says Judy. "The love of a mother and daughter is a very special gift from above. To God be the glory for stepping in and guiding me to write the memories without my knowing that my dear, sweet mother would soon be gone."

Judy's mother eventually contracted pneumonia and passed away at age eighty-six. She left a beautiful legacy in the hearts and minds of five children, thirteen grandchildren, eighteen great-grandchildren, and four great-great-grandchildren. Judy spoke at her funeral, and said in part: "Our mother taught us to love others. She loved her children, her grandchildren, and her great-grandchildren. She also loved her neighbors. She was a mother who taught us all the words and the meaning of John 15:17: 'This is my command: Love each other.'"

Judy knows that God clearly answered a desire of her heart, to somehow express to her mother the deep, abiding love she had always felt for her. Now she has more than the memories—she has a written record to share with her own children and grandchildren.

FIFTEEN

With This Ring

I will repay you for the years the locusts have eaten.

—JOEL 2:25

"Your engagement ring is beautiful," said Laura's manicurist.

Laura tried to still the butterflies that took flight every time she glanced down at her finger. "Thank you. Today I'll be adding the matching wedding ring."

In a few short hours, her ring finger would declare to the world that she was a married woman. Her mind drifted back to the other ring she'd worn on that finger when she was a teenager—a lovely opal she'd received from her mother on her sixteenth birthday. She longed to wear it on this, her wedding day, as a symbol of "something old." But unfortunately, that was not possible.

During a trip several years earlier, she'd carefully wrapped her opal ring in a soft tissue, then tucked it into her suede purse for safekeeping. However, when she arrived home, the ring was missing. Laura searched every square inch of the purse, including ripping out the lining, but had to accept the inevitable: her treasured ring was gone.

Laura mentioned the opal ring to the manicurist, who offered an encouraging word. "Don't worry. These things have a way of turning up. I bet you'll find it before the ceremony."

Laura wasn't so sure. Years of searching and praying had not turned up a single clue. "Over time, reminders of the ring would emerge and I'd drag the purse out of the closet for yet another search. And each time I'd remind God how precious that ring was to me: 'Lord, I cherish this sweet-sixteen birthday present from my mom. As a single parent, this ring was a financial sacrifice for her. Please, I'm begging you—make it appear.' But it never did."

An ongoing search for the ring proved fruitless. Sometimes she grew so frustrated, she'd toss the old, worn purse into the trash, only to retrieve it within minutes. Something held her to the dream of finding the ring. If she kept praying, she figured it might miraculously appear someday.

So there she sat on the verge of getting married, fixed once more on the memory of her mother's long-lost gift. She glanced again at her engagement ring and reasoned, *A glittering wedding ring will soon replace the ring I lost. That will be more than enough.*

For a year and a half, married life was blissful. Her bubble burst one day, though, when her husband announced that he wanted out of his commitment. "Sorrow welled within me like a tidal wave," recalls Laura. "It was pure agony to remove my wedding ring."

Once again, her ring finger was bare—a constant reminder of her broken heart. She wept for months. Finally, when a friend invited her to go on a shopping trip, she jumped at the opportunity. She needed a sense of normalcy again.

> ONCE AGAIN, HER RING FINGER WAS BARE— A CONSTANT REMINDER OF HER BROKEN HEART.

"For some bizarre reason, I decided to use that old suede purse," Laura reflects. "Perhaps it was just a reminder of sweeter times." She tucked her lipstick and her wallet into the purse, along with a few other items.

Only God could have orchestrated what happened next.

While chatting with her friend, she reached into her purse for a tissue, but the one she pulled out was used, wadded up into a tiny ball. Within moments, she was shedding happy tears as she discovered the missing opal ring inside. *How could I have missed it all those years?*

she wondered. *Why hadn't it turned up during my countless searches?*

She'll never forget the moment she slid the treasured opal back onto her finger. Like a mother tenderly drawing an injured child close, she felt the Lord comforting her, assuring her that while others may desert her, he would never leave her side.

How fitting it was that God should choose a ring to symbolize his faithfulness and steadfast love. How amazing, too, that he should choose a moment in Laura's life when she felt at her lowest—worthless and unlovable. Through the perfectly timed discovery, God's message rang out loud and clear: *Don't worry. I am busy taking care of every last detail. You are mine and I am yours.*

Laura's ring reminds her of her sixteenth birthday, when she was young and carefree. It also turns her thoughts toward eternity. She imagines the moment she'll meet her Savior face-to-face, as described in I Peter 5:4: "When the Chief Shepherd appears, you will receive the crown of glory that will never fade away."

"When I get to Heaven and Jesus bestows my crown on me, I wonder if it will be adorned with opal," says Laura.

Whatever the gem, she's certain of this: she'll humbly bow before him and lay that crown of glory at his feet.

Highway to Holland

I love to live on the brink of eternity.

—DAVID BRAINERD

Kathy sipped a hazelnut cappuccino as she eased onto the highway ramp between Holland and Grand Rapids. The normal five o'clock traffic rushed past. She was heading to class and didn't have time to spare.

Halfway to Grand Rapids, she heard a loud, rhythmic, *bump-bump-bump* sound. About the same time, her car veered to the side as if it were being tugged. She pulled over and discovered a flat tire. She had never changed a flat; she was going to be late for class. Her mind raced to remember what a person should do when stranded on a busy highway. She didn't have a cell phone, so calling for help was out of the question.

Keeping one eye on cars flying past, she raised the hood, turned on the emergency blinkers, and placed a sign in her back window where someone might see it. It read, "CALL POLICE" in large, red, block letters.

To add to her anxiety, darkness was fast approaching. A still, small voice inside her head advised her to step back inside her car and calm down. "I was pretty sure the voice belonged to God," says Kathy. How did God expect her to to be calm at that stressful moment?

"Lord, I know you've always said you'd never leave me. I choose to believe that. I'll try my best to calm down," she prayed.

> A STILL, SMALL VOICE INSIDE HER HEAD ADVISED HER TO STEP BACK INSIDE HER CAR AND CALM DOWN.

Her cup of coffee was still warm and tasted unusually good. "My favorite Christian songs were playing on the radio, and I could feel myself starting to relax."

A couple of minutes later, a car pulled over and parked behind her. "I didn't know whether I should be happy or lock my doors." She glanced back to see two women who looked to be in their fifties. Kathy figured they looked harmless, so she stepped out of her car and made her way back to theirs.

The driver pointed to a spot across the highway. "We were heading to Holland and saw you from over there," she said. "We couldn't pass you by without checking to see if you needed help."

The women offered Kathy a ride to the next gas station, so she settled into their cozy, leather backseat and thanked them for coming to her rescue.

"Want to call anyone?" they asked, handing her a cell phone. She phoned her husband and her school to let them know what had happened.

"Those women were joyful!" says Kathy. "They said they were sisters who often traveled together and that they loved a good adventure. I found myself enjoying their company."

They pulled into a service station, where an attendant offered to pick up Kathy's car and tow it back to the station to fix the tire. He said it would take a couple of hours to complete, because of their heavy workload. He showed her to a lobby where she could wait.

Kathy hugged the two sisters good-bye and thanked them again. She had just begun to read a magazine when their white car pulled back into the parking lot. They'd returned with an offer Kathy couldn't refuse. "We can't just leave you sitting here for two hours. We're going your way, so why don't we just drive you home?" they asked.

Touched by their generous offer, Kathy accepted the ride back to Holland. The three of them spent the time sharing how God's goodness had touched their lives. The ride turned into a time of thanksgiving and praise.

"When we pulled into my driveway, I wrote their names and addresses on a piece of paper so I could send them a thank-you card later," says Kathy. "My husband suggested we go pick up the car, so I was still able to make part of my class."

When Kathy walked into class, her teacher asked, "Didn't you say you had a flat tire tonight?"

"Yes, just west of the 44th Street overpass."

He looked confused. "That's really strange. You and Dave are the only ones who live in Holland and who use that highway to travel to class. Dave left a message that said he too had a flat tire tonight, except his tire blew on the east side of the 44th Street exit. A carload of teenagers picked him up, which was great, because he says it gave him an opportunity to share the gospel with them."

KATHY'S EYES OPENED WIDE TO GOD'S BIGGER PICTURE.

Kathy's eyes opened wide to God's bigger picture. "If I hadn't had a flat tire, I would have stopped to pick Dave up to bring him to class." She recognized the purpose behind that night's events. Those teens were supposed to pick Dave up so he could share God's good news with them.

"God took care of me by calming me down with music

and a warm drink, and he sent two highway 'angels' to rescue me at just the right time." At the same time, he was busy arranging help for Dave.

Kathy concludes, "His perfect timing taught me a huge lesson in trust."

Shy No More

The Lord will fulfill his purpose for me.

—PSALM 138:8

Sixteen-year-old Laura leaned against the wall of her church at the exact spot where she stood every single week and poured out her heart to God. *I'm so sick of being alone! Why can't I start a conversation the way other people do?*

She'd tried her best to fit in with her church youth group, but nothing worked. "It felt like torture being the wallflower of the group," Laura remembers. "I felt stuck in an endless cycle of rejection and tears. Loneliness, bitterness, and depression had become the norm for me. I found it easier to turn away from God than to face my problem."

Her problem intensified to the point where she wondered whether life was worth living. One day, while the youth worship team sang their closing song, she silently prayed, *Lord, get me out of this mess. Help me!*

A few minutes later, Pastor Ted walked up to her. He looked concerned. "Are you OK, Laura—really OK?" he asked.

Laura crossed her arms and whispered, "I honestly don't know anymore."

His compassion pierced her pain. "Let's talk."

IT FELT GOOD TO CONFESS HER SECRET— BUT HOW WOULD THAT CHANGE ANYTHING?

Laura described how heartbroken and alone she felt, and how it was sending her into a downward spiral. "I hate the feeling of always being depressed," she confided. It felt good to confess her secret—but how would that change anything?

"Laura, I'm going to make a bold proposition," said Pastor Ted as he looked her in the eye. "Are you ready to hear what I have to say?"

She swallowed hard and nodded.

"You've memorized Bible verses since you were a little girl. Well, now you're going to have to put them to work. I want you to step out into the water in faith and walk.

Either you can do all things through Christ, or God is a liar. Which is it?"

God—a liar? How could that be true? Walk on water? How am I supposed to do that? Laura wondered.

Pastor Ted took it a step further. "Let me ask you something. Why don't you talk to people?"

Laura cringed at the question. "I just . . . can't. I don't know how to start a conversation."

Pastor Ted's expression brightened. "Well, I have an idea. Next week, I want you to go up to people and compliment them. Ask them where they got their shoes. Ask them questions."

Laura weighed his words carefully. *Maybe I could try it,* she thought.

Pastor Ted continued, "I think what you need, Laura, is an extreme makeover. Make some major changes in your life and see what happens. With God's help, I'm sure you can do it."

The very mention of an extreme makeover grabbed her attention. No more excuses! From that point on, she couldn't waste time sitting around wishing she had friends; Pastor Ted's assignment was going to force her to get out there and find friends. In fact, a makeover that extreme might even change her entire life.

"That night at home, I made a list," says Laura. "First,

my attitude toward people had to change. All that fear in my heart had to be cast away. It was time to step out and take a risk."

Laura then decided that she needed to make some outward changes as well. The first change took place when she cut eight inches off her waist-length hair. Add to that some makeup and a new outfit, and she felt different already. She checked herself over in the mirror and thought, *The kids at youth group won't know what hit 'em.*

Her first time back at youth group was unforgettable. When she breezed into church, she noticed a girl who was sitting alone. Laura thought instantly of Philippians 4:13, "I can do everything through him who gives me strength." God used that verse as fuel, and with a burst of newfound confidence, she walked right up to the girl and heard herself say, "Hi! What's up?"

> IN THE FOLLOWING MONTHS, LAURA'S RELATIONSHIP WITH GOD DEEPENED.

"We only had a short conversation, but for me it was huge. Up to that moment, my life had been all about caution and reducing risks, but no more. Jesus held me up and filled me with courage, strength—and words!"

In the following months, Laura's relationship with God deepened. She attended summer camp and group Bible studies and gradually discovered what it was like to have a real social life. She learned how it felt to belong to a group of trusted friends. At one point, a friend commented that Laura was "the most talkative shy person ever!"

Today Laura marvels at how God has transformed her life. "Once I surrendered my struggles, the shyness faded away." God changed her from a quiet, almost invisible girl to a strong young lady with a voice.

Laura discovered that God has a sense of humor too. When a friend nicknamed her Motormouth, she knew she'd won the battle over timidity.

In the Midst of Chaos

People see God every day; they just don't recognize him.

—PEARL BUCK

Shots fired! Few things can get a reporter moving and fill his heart with dread faster than hearing those two words. The phrase usually means that a lead story is in the making for the next newspaper edition or TV newscast.

It also means a human tragedy has begun to unfold.

Those words stopped reporter Thomas Smith in his tracks one Friday afternoon. He'd just arrived for his weekend shift at a midsize daily newspaper in South Carolina. He recalls, "A woman at the front counter was telling the head of circulation about traffic being rerouted just down the street. I half-listened to the conversation as I checked the fax machine. She said there were local police, deputies, and highway patrol cars everywhere."

As if on cue, the newsroom scanner broadcast those two chilling words: *shots fired.*

AS IF ON CUE, THE NEWSROOM SCANNER BROADCAST THOSE TWO CHILLING WORDS: SHOTS FIRED.

As the dispatcher relayed bits and pieces of the breaking events, the horror of the situation revealed itself full force. Someone had gone on a shooting rampage at a nearby parts manufacturing plant. Voices crackled through the scanner speaker as various law enforcement agencies radioed in while taking their positions around the building.

Thomas ran to the city editor's office and said, "Kelly, there's been a shooting at the plant. I'm on the way now." Heading toward the newsroom door, he called back over his shoulder, "Send me a photographer as soon as you can."

Kelly was already on the phone, paging the newsroom's chief photographer.

The plant was about a mile from the newspaper office, and Thomas realized halfway there that a man with good sense would be heading away from the shooting, not toward it. He checked his microcassette recorder to make sure it was working OK, then rewound the tape. As he rounded the curve leading to the parking lot of the plant, he glanced at the visor on the passenger's side of the truck. Sure enough, he'd clipped an extra reporter's notepad and pen there, as always.

Thomas found the parking lot had been cordoned off, so he pulled onto the shoulder of the road, a safe distance away. "I was the first media person on the scene," he says. "On the hill above me, about two hundred and fifty people milled about in shock, watching the building across the road. They were the second shift workers who had been evacuated from the building when the shooting started."

> EVEN IN THAT CHAOTIC SCENE, PLANT MANAGERS HAD SOMEHOW MANAGED TO EVACUATE AN ENTIRE SHIFT SAFELY IN LESS THAN FIVE MINUTES.

Even in that chaotic scene, plant managers had somehow managed to evacuate an entire shift safely in less than five minutes. Thomas studied them for a long moment, then walked over to speak with the public affairs liaison for the sheriff's department. They met at the edge of the parking lot.

"Tom, you're a little too close to the building," said the liaison. "This guy is armed and he may start shooting again any minute."

Thomas agreed to join the folks up on the hill, but first requested a quick update. A couple of photographers and a second reporter arrived as he received the information. He learned that a former employee had returned to the plant after having been dismissed a month earlier. Before entering the building, he'd shot the security guard in the booth out front, cut the phone lines, then headed straight for the personnel department and opened fire. When he noticed people attempting to escape, he'd turned his rage on them.

> THOMAS INSTINCTIVELY REACHED IN HIS POCKET FOR THE RECORDER, THEN REALIZED THAT IT WAS NOT A GOOD TIME FOR COLLECTING QUOTES.

"By the time the building was empty—five minutes later—seven people were either wounded or dead," recalls Thomas. "My job was to talk to people and get their reaction to the events. At one point, a man walked up and said his son was one of those who had been shot. He needed to know if he was dead or alive." The man was willing to be interviewed at that stressful moment if it meant finding out the status of his son.

Thomas instinctively reached in his pocket for the recorder, then realized that it was not a good time for collecting quotes. Instead, he led the worried father to the officer he had spoken with earlier and explained the situation. He left them and headed for the hill, but at one point, glanced behind in time to see "that bear of a man" gently holding a heartbroken father in his arms.

Thomas recalls a most unusual moment. "As I listened to the stories from people who had just run through hell trying to find safety, people who couldn't account for family members who worked at the plant, and people who came within inches of being the shooter's next victim, I heard a sound. It started softly."

Just one voice.

Then others joined in. "Amazing grace, how sweet the sound . . ."

Even in the midst of chaos, God is there.

A Dream Restored

Whenever the sounds of the world die out in the soul, or sink low,
then we hear these whisperings of God. He is always
whispering to us, only we do not always hear, because of the noise,
hurry, and distraction which life causes as it rushes on.

—FREDERICK W. FABER

Walking on the beach, Maureen stoops to pick up a seashell. Sun glints off her bracelet and distracts her momentarily. There under glass is a photo of two boys, plus two tiny pearls rolling free inside the charm. The pearls symbolize purpose from pain and beauty from brokenness after a long journey to motherhood. Her eyes brim with tears as she recalls the beginning of her heart's deepest longing.

"Mommy, will I have a baby someday?" she had asked,

tenderly holding her doll like a mother cradles her child. The maternal instinct that tugged at Maureen's young heart was like the seed of a dream that would later fully blossom.

> THE MATERNAL INSTINCT THAT TUGGED AT MAUREEN'S YOUNG HEART WAS LIKE THE SEED OF A DREAM THAT WOULD LATER FULLY BLOSSOM.

"But little did I know that this dream would cause both heartache and joy," says Maureen.

Childhood melted into the teen years and dating became a heated issue. "Mother! Can't I stay out later?" Maureen would argue. Her parents' curfew never seemed to mesh with her plans for the evening. "The movie doesn't start until ten. Can't you bend the rules just this once?"

Maureen searched her mother's face for clues and wondered if she suspected the truth. Did she know that Maureen's relationship with her boyfriend had become more than casual?

There was no negotiating curfew.

Maureen clearly recalls the day she held a pregnancy test in her hand. The result had read "inconclusive."

"In my heart I believed that sex before marriage wasn't right," says Maureen. But she had let the desire for physical love overrule her convictions. Even so, she wasn't ready for her boyfriend's gruff and shocking announcement: "If you're pregnant, you'll have to have an abortion."

The maternal feelings she'd experienced as a little girl bubbled to the surface. *Kill my baby—our baby? Never!* "How could you even suggest that?" she shouted back. "Is that what our relationship means to you?"

"We're not ready to be parents," her boyfriend reminded her. "Just think how our lives would change."

Maureen couldn't believe what she was hearing. "How our lives would change? We've already been living like a married couple! I can't believe how selfish you are! We both knew the risks, but chose to play the game."

Her boyfriend wouldn't hear of it. "You're the one who's being selfish!"

It was an emotional tug-of-war. "The battle between us raged—each of us standing our ground," says Maureen. "We were scared, and though we would soon learn that I wasn't pregnant, our words that day would later return to haunt us."

THE BATTLE BETWEEN US RAGED—EACH OF US STANDING OUR GROUND.

"'Mommy, I love you!' How I'd longed to hear those words," remembers Maureen. "But instead, I heard my doctor telling me that I would never be able to have children."

She and her boyfriend had married by then, and her doctor's news sent her thoughts tumbling back to their long-ago argument. She couldn't help but wonder if God was punishing them for the life they'd lived as teens.

You know that I wouldn't have had an abortion! she prayed. *Please, please don't punish us.* It felt like her heart was breaking.

Maureen had grown close to her mother through the years. She shared her devastating news and asked, "Mom, will you agree with me in prayer?"

With her mother at her side, she gave her dream of motherhood back to God. "You know me better than I know myself. Your Word says that if I'll delight myself in the Lord, you'll give me the desire of my heart. So I hand you my dream, and I trust you to work it out in your own way."

> ALTHOUGH GOD HAD CHOSEN NOT TO GIVE HER A CHILD, HE HELPED SOOTHE HER DISAPPOINTMENT UNTIL SHE FOUND PEACE WITHIN.

Months passed. Maureen underwent a transformation that she would never have believed. Although God had chosen not to give her a child, he helped soothe her disappointment until she found peace within. One day while talking to her mother, she described the huge change that had come over her.

"God has spoken to my heart lately in such amazing, tender ways, Mom. Even though I gave my dream back to him to do as he sees fit, he seems to be asking me to just sit still and trust him."

She had claimed a special Scripture, Ecclesiastes 3:11,

where it speaks of God making all things beautiful in his good time. Whatever God wanted was what Maureen wanted. And so she waited.

"Mommy! Mommy!" Maureen's two sons have joined her on the beach.

"Over eight years have passed since God fulfilled my deepest longing," she says happily, "and then eighteen months later, he brought us a third son as an answer to our prayers. Our children were born from other women's pain and heartbreak, yet those women chose life—sacrificing to give us these precious gifts."

God's gifts often arrive in packages different from what we anticipate. He delights in delivering them at a time that will leave the most lasting impact. God answered Maureen's childhood prayer by introducing three beautiful children into her life when she needed them most.

TWENTY

The Christmas Star

When they saw the star, they were overjoyed.

—MATTHEW 2:10

From the time she was a little girl, Lori adored Christmas. Filled with a sense of awe and wonder, she adored everything about that holy day: the amazing sights, sounds, and smells. "Christmas Day itself felt almost magical," recalls Lori. She remembers believing that anything at all was possible on that special day. She was certain that every dream was within her reach.

And that's not all.

"Christmas taught me the importance of giving and receiving, and how sometimes the greatest gifts are not those that can be held, but those that are only seen in our minds and felt with our hearts."

Lori grew up in a large family on a farm in rural Kansas. As is the case with most families her size, finances were often tight. "My father worked long hours as a repairman for a small, independent telephone company. He was also a farmer, reaping and sowing both good years and bad, with the help of my mother."

Her mother's world revolved around their home, where she devoted her time to their six children. "She made our world sing."

Holidays were always special, but nothing extravagant. Her mother worked to make them simple and sweet. They'd cut a cedar tree from the edge of their pasture, line up their freshly baked sugar cookies on wax paper, and exchange gifts that Lori describes as "wrapped with love."

The entire month of December generated an unforgettable excitement, but the most memorable Christmas Day event happened around 1970. That Christmas, Lori says her family received a surprise long before the sun rose, a "sign of hope and a message of ultimate love."

She was eight or nine, snuggled under the covers on Christmas Eve. The night was cold and frosty, and as usual, she and her sister were filled to the brim with anticipation. They shared a room upstairs and lay there in the dark, whispering about what might be tucked under the tree in the room directly below.

It was still dark outside when Lori felt her mother's hand gently tapping her shoulder. Mom spoke softly, telling the girls to grab their robes and meet her downstairs. "It was far too early for us to be getting up for breakfast or gathering in the living room to open gifts," says Lori.

SIBYL, THEIR NEIGHBOR DOWN THE STREET, HAD PHONED WITH NEWS ABOUT A STAR.

She and her sister exchanged bewildered looks and did as their mother instructed. After awakening their brothers, the girls joined the whole family, gathered outside on their twilight mission. Sibyl, their neighbor down the street, had phoned with news about a star.

"So my family and I stood on the steps of our back porch, huddling close for warmth. There, right above the eastern horizon, we saw it—a large, extremely bright star. The star shone like a beacon, a perfect crystal against a crisp, clear curtain of midnight," she remembers. "Sleepy eyes and young hearts opened wide in wonder."

That sacred moment is forever etched in Lori's memory, because she shared the spectacular sight with the people most dear to her heart—her family. "It was the ultimate Christmas greeting, a living card that held a message for the whole world."

It was also the beginning of a sense of reverence and awe, which would draw her ever closer to God in the years to come.

Every Christmas after that initial sighting, Lori would awaken long before dawn to creep out to the porch and search the sky again. Age didn't hinder her search. "I continued my quest, gazing into the early morning every Christmas for the same bright star that shone outside the back door of our small Kansas farm."

She has yet to locate a brilliant star like the one she witnessed on that special night. "Sometimes I wonder if I might have only imagined it, and yet my whole family remembers the event in detail."

Lori has decided that their family must have needed some sort of reminder of God's steadfast love on that particular Christmas. "His star was our very first gift that Christmas morning, and it has remained the most beautiful and enduring gift of all, as I remember it each year."

> HIS STAR WAS OUR VERY FIRST GIFT THAT CHRISTMAS MORNING, AND IT HAS REMAINED THE MOST BEAUTIFUL AND ENDURING GIFT OF ALL, AS I REMEMBER IT EACH YEAR.

Several years have passed since Lori tiptoed to the edge of dawn in search of the Christmas star. "The message it left behind still speaks as clearly to me now as it did when I was a little girl," says Lori. "I will always believe in the glorious birth of Jesus and in the star that still beckons us all to follow his light."

TWENTY-ONE

A New Way of Seeing

The bridge of grace will bear your weight.

—CHARLES SPURGEON

I n the beginning, Regina was too young to realize she was blind. Born two months early, she was a fragile baby. Her mother knew there would be great challenges ahead.

"She prayed in faith, and she sheltered me. The first few years of my life are a complete blur—literally. I only remember sounds, smells, and textures." Regina describes her vision as "shadows in color."

"To see or not to see—that was the question," says Regina. "I wanted to see."

Long before she understood what was wrong, though, her mother taught her to pray. "Whenever we prayed for my eyes to get better, I would think, *What's she talking about? My eyes aren't sick! They're not coughing or sneezing.*"

God had blessed her with a mother who never thought of her daughter as disabled. She treated her the same way she treated everybody else. "It wasn't until it was time to go to school that I realized I was different from other children."

Regina attended public school, where she had to sit at the front of the class in order to see the chalkboard. School introduced her to teasing. Her schoolmates chattered about things she couldn't see. "They talked about my glasses too, which I'd been wearing since I was eighteen months old." Until that moment, she hadn't realized that her glasses were considered ugly, so she didn't understand the children's snide remarks and laughter. She began praying for God to take away her need for glasses.

The glasses remained. In the following years, Regina experienced emotional turmoil that taught her to guard her true feelings. She learned to laugh with those who belittled her, but spent her days crying on the inside. She also questioned God: *What did I do to be born this way, Lord?*

Eventually, she learned to accept her plight. "Even though I couldn't see, I could still do what others did," says Regina. "I believed that one day I would see. In my dreams, I never wore glasses."

At age thirteen, Regina became a seamstress in spite

of her limited vision. She sewed even though some believed at first that she wouldn't be able to thread a needle. She had determination and figured, "I can feel the hole in the needle even though I can't see it."

Whenever she reviews her past, Regina always credits her mother's faith for bringing about the change in her. It would be many years before she learned the reason for her lack of clear vision. "During my junior year in college, I ran across an article on early childhood development, and learned that many premature babies born in the late forties and early fifties were either blind or legally blind because of the lights that were used in their incubators. The lights had burned their retinas." She thanked God for showing her that her vision problem wasn't somehow her fault.

THE BEST PART OF ALL IS THE INTENTIONAL PATH GOD SMOOTHED FOR HER FROM THE VERY BEGINNING.

Over thirty years passed. By then, Regina still wore glasses, but she had heard about a doctor who specialized in contact lenses. After a detailed exam, he determined that her left eye could not be helped, but seemed certain that he could create a lens to correct her right eye. The income she made from her sewing made the procedure affordable.

Two wedding gown contracts later, she had enough money to buy her contacts.

"Are we ever satisfied when we get what we want?" Regina asks. "I wanted to see without having to wear glasses. Contact lenses made that possible. But was I satisfied? No. I continued praying for 20/20 vision."

Fast-forward to age forty-seven. Regina underwent LASIK eye surgery to correct her vision. Once again it was her sewing—God's gift of a reliable income—that made it possible for her to afford the surgery. Now, at fifty-five, she has enjoyed almost perfect vision for eight years.

"My doctor is still amazed at how well I have done," says Regina. "My right eye sees 20/20, and the left eye, which I didn't use before, now sees 20/50 or better."

The best part of all is the intentional path God smoothed for her from the very beginning. "It took forty-seven years to weave together my mother's faith, our prayers, my sewing, and my doctor's knowledge and skills to provide this miracle of sight. For this I praise God every day!"

TWENTY-TWO

The Gift of Poetry

*Just as a servant knows that he must first obey
his master in all things, so the surrender to an implicit and
unquestionable obedience must become the
essential characteristic of our lives.*

—ANDREW MURRAY

One of the amazing ways God works is by bringing strangers across our paths and then using our gifts to help them. One Sunday morning, Nanette met one such stranger at her church.

After the service ended, she noticed a young woman standing across the church sanctuary. Hanging from one of her arms was a polished wooden cane. Nanette greeted her with a friendly handshake and recalls how cold the woman's hands felt. Her skin had a peculiar yellow tinge, and sad, sunken eyes pointed to some sort of chronic illness.

Nanette's heart went out to her, and she thought of her often. However, she only saw her at church once more after their initial meeting. By that time, Nanette had found out that the woman's name was Renita. Renita was losing a valiant battle with kidney disease. As her health continued to worsen, she could no longer attend church.

"My heart broke for this young woman, and I wanted to do something to ease her suffering," says Nanette. "Others took food and visited her, but I wanted to give food that wouldn't perish. I decided to provide food for her soul."

Nanette hesitated at first. She didn't want to add to Renita's burden, but felt it was a sacred act to reach out to those who suffer. She longed to touch Renita's life, just as if her own hands and feet belonged to Jesus.

> SHE LONGED TO TOUCH RENITA'S LIFE, JUST AS IF HER OWN HANDS AND FEET BELONGED TO JESUS.

One Sunday, Renita showed up unexpectedly at church. Her skin had turned a deeper shade of yellow, and it looked as though the light in her eyes had grown dim. Nanette sensed an urgency to act.

Earlier in the year, she had published a booklet of vignettes and poetry. "I borrowed the following poem from my book, typed it up, and framed it for Renita. Though it wasn't written for anyone in particular, I prayed it would touch her and heal any broken places in her heart," says Nanette.

ABIDING

I feel like the rose, Lord,
After the blush of spring
Has left the petals,
Turned them brown—
Wilted.

The petals are torn away
One by one,
Like pieces of my life,
Drifting aimlessly,
On the wind.

I pray for the ability
To pull the rose
Back together
Into a tiny bud—
To begin again.

Day by day, I'll see
The bud open,
Spread its petals,
Kiss the sunshine
And the dew.

In Your gentle hands,
Lord, I'll be that rose
On the vine called love,
And I'll abide in You,
And You in me.

Several months later, Renita's mother approached Nanette before a church service was to begin. "Every time I visit Renita's house, I see your poem sitting on the table next to her bed." Nanette was pleased to hear that Renita liked her poem, but thought, *I can't believe one little poem means so much to her.*

> EVERY TIME I VISIT
> RENITA'S HOUSE,
> I SEE YOUR POEM SITTING
> ON THE TABLE
> NEXT TO HER BED.

Life took them in different directions, and Nanette and Renita no longer attended the same church. As sometimes happens in such situations, Nanette rarely thought about Renita anymore. But she continued to share her poems with the ill or with those who had experienced a loss. Although she never looked for thanks, over the years a select few returned to express their gratitude.

Barbara was a friend who helped Nanette print the poetry she gave away as gifts. One day while working together, Barbara received a phone call. Nanette continued with her work, taking pains to frame her poetry just so.

Barbara was listening intently to the person on the line. "I'm so sorry," she said, her voice trailing off. She held her hand over the receiver and whispered to Nanette, "A friend of mine has died from kidney disease."

Nanette asked for the friend's name.

"Renita."

Nanette later explained how Renita had touched her heart, though they'd met only briefly.

GOD TOOK HER GIFT OF POETRY AND USED HER WORDS TO BRING COMFORT TO EVERYONE WHO ATTENDED RENITA'S MEMORIAL SERVICE.

"Would you like to go to her memorial service?" Barbara asked.

Nanette declined. She didn't know Renita well and didn't want to impose on a service meant for family and close friends. But after the service, she received a call from Barbara.

"Nan, you won't believe what happened! They read your poem at Renita's memorial service."

That news convinced Nanette that there's joy in giving that can extend even to the last day of a person's life. God took her gift of poetry and used her words to bring comfort to everyone who attended Renita's memorial service.

Like the rose that blooms anew each year, in God's hands one little poem may keep on bringing comfort and joy again and again.

Stuck in Surrey

*The peace of God, which transcends all understanding, will guard
your hearts and your minds in Christ Jesus.*

—PHILIPPIANS 4:6, 7

Violet reread the newsy letter from a friend who had
been living in Hong Kong for the past ten months
on a two-year teaching assignment. The letter sounded
like a lively travelogue, with amusing descriptions of
misadventures in the marketplace when she'd tried using
her halting grasp of Cantonese. She described her family's
Christmas as well, when they'd toured mainland China.
Next Christmas they were planning to tour Vietnam,
and as soon as the school year dismissed, she said, they
planned to camp in China's Wu Han province.

Violet stared at the blinking cursor on her computer
screen. What could she possibly say in reply to a letter

like that? Her own summer plans were hardly exciting. "After nearly a year without a job, my husband, Ernie, was starting his second month of a six-month work contract. Our money situation was tight, and I knew unemployment could strike again."

There would be no lazy weeks traveling to visit family or camping in their tent trailer by pristine lakes or pine forests. "I was stuck in Surrey," says Violet.

> THERE WOULD BE NO LAZY WEEKS TRAVELING TO VISIT FAMILY OR CAMPING IN THEIR TENT TRAILER BY PRISTINE LAKES OR PINE FORESTS.

She recalled the day about a month earlier when she'd first heard Ernie's startling phone announcement: "I'll be home early. I'm finished here."

Her emotions struggled from panic to peace and plummeted to panic again as the reality of their situation sank in. She brooded over questions about the length of Ernie's severance package and whether they'd be able to survive on her part-time pay. Would they have to move?

Sometimes Violet felt a spark of excitement as she considered their new challenges ahead. But at other times, when the only response to numerous job applications was silence, or when Ernie's few interviews did not yield a callback, she felt like God had abandoned them.

She felt weary, overwhelmed at times by worry. God

reminded her of her favorite Bible promise: "Do not be anxious about anything, but in everything, by prayer and petition, with thanksgiving, present your requests to God. And the peace of God, which transcends all understanding, will guard your hearts and your minds in Christ Jesus" (Philippians 4:6, 7).

"I repeated those verses every time anxiety reared its head," remembers Violet. "Then I once again relinquished my husband's job situation to God." It was the only way to regain a certain measure of tranquility. Finally, after eleven months without work, Ernie found a short-term job. It was a welcome relief to them both.

Then the letter arrived from her friend in Hong Kong, making Violet's life sound dreary and disappointing by comparison. Violet felt sucked into a whirlpool of discontent and sat at her computer unable to type a single word.

Fresh air would do her good, she thought, so she set off on her usual brisk morning walk through the park. "The day was too sunny for my sour mood," recalls Violet. "Instead of hearing the birds singing along the path, a tired cliché sprang to the beat of my footsteps: 'Been here. Done this.' Listening to my favorite music didn't help much either."

Violet had reached her usual turning point on the path—a weeping willow that marked her return home—when a song in her headphones lifted her gloom.

Though she'd heard the song dozens of times before, at that moment it felt like she was hearing it for the very first time. The words spoke of how difficult it was to wait when things weren't clear and how wonderful it is to learn to love the dreams God has for us. The song ended with a commitment to listen to God and to stay exactly where he has placed us until he moves us on.

The song's lyrics were riveting, and she played it again. Violet felt as if God had laid his hand on her shoulder as a reminder to submit her discontent to his care. "Though his plans for me might not include exotic travel or even the summer vacation to which I was accustomed, I knew I was standing where he had lovingly led me," she reveals. "He was asking me whether I was going to give in to envy and self-pity or keep trusting him, even in an uncertain, disappointing season."

During her return home, Violet committed to trusting God, no matter what. At that moment of decision, her eyes took in the beauty of swaying grass and morning sunlight, shining through the petals of a flower.

Though her summer plans hadn't changed, the fog of discontent had evaporated under the warmth of God's timely touch. The words of a simple song had ministered to her, and she continued her sunny walk home in perfect peace.

She no longer felt stuck in Surrey.

A Glimpse of the Sacred

Next to faith this is the highest art—
to be content with the calling in which God has placed you.

—MARTIN LUTHER

Sharon enjoyed teaching, but remembers her thir-teenth year of working with first graders as one filled with challenges she hadn't faced before. "Day after day, I faced wiggly and sometimes unruly boys and girls. My gift of being able to draw out and tame the difficult child earned me a class filled with students who had special needs. But no one challenged me more than Joey."

Joey was tough even at six years of age. He had experienced abandonment, abuse, and trauma that no one should ever have to endure. "I'll never forget how he sauntered into the room on the first day, proudly displaying his arrogance and toughness," remarks Sharon.

His classmates sized him up and quickly sensed their differences. "Although I sought ways to sow seeds of love in his heart, it seemed he'd purposely thwart all of my attempts. For instance, although at the end of each day I shook the hands of my children and even offered hugs if they wanted them, Joey stiffly refused any form of physical contact."

His childlike trust had been broken, and he was understandably wary of that happening again. He'd lean stiffly away from her, and it would pierce her heart with a deep sadness. She ached to be a source of healing in his young life, but that seemed like an unreachable dream.

> SHE ACHED TO BE A SOURCE OF HEALING IN HIS YOUNG LIFE, BUT THAT SEEMED LIKE AN UNREACHABLE DREAM.

Fall turned to winter, and Joey was showing small signs of improvement. Sharon spent countless hours working to connect with him. They studied insects together and pored over dinosaur bones. She brought turtles to school too. "He seemed more relaxed with me by then," she remembers, "and sometimes I'd catch his eyes smiling. But every afternoon as my students walked past me on the way out of class, Joey would lower his head and stiffen his back. His body clearly shouted 'Keep away!'"

By the time spring arrived, Sharon had wearied in her attempt to love this tough student. "But Joey tugged at my heartstrings. He represented so many hurting children in the world. I found that I just couldn't give up."

By the time spring arrived, Sharon had wearied in her attempt to love this tough student.

She did notice that Joey was starting to relax more with the other boys and girls. And he approached her more easily now. She looked forward to him racing into the classroom each morning to share something interesting with her. "His belligerence had faded and his eyes had softened. He began to show signs of leadership too. I praised each step in the right direction."

The school year was drawing to a close long before Sharon was ready to release Joey into the next grade. When June arrived, Sharon says her heart longed to shield and protect him. "I wanted to continue building on his obvious strengths. But time was running out. The 180-day school year seemed much too short for children like Joey, who needed a healthy attachment to a safe person."

On their last afternoon together, she asked her class to line up at the door as usual. One by one the students passed her and she wished them well. She gave pats on the back, an occasional hug, or gentle handshakes.

Some children clung to her as if they didn't want to let go of the school year.

When it was Joey's turn, Sharon felt her heart thumping. She made a point of looking deep into his eyes, and she recalls that for once, he did not lower his head.

WHAT HAPPENED NEXT WAS LIKE A MIRACLE UNFOLDING BEFORE HER EYES.

"You've done well, Joey. I'm proud of you," she told him.

He tossed her a shy smile in return. "Bye, Miss Brani," he said softly. She watched him amble out the door.

At the last minute, he hesitated as if something were blocking his exit.

What happened next was like a miracle unfolding before her eyes. Joey turned suddenly to face her. "He threw his long arms around me and buried his face in my embrace. I felt his body sobbing," says Sharon.

"Thanks, Miss Brani," he mumbled tearfully. He paused a moment before stepping back into line and out the door.

Sharon's eyes brimmed with tears. "I believe in you, Joey," she called to him. "I always will."

Joey had already reached the end of the hall. He turned one more time and waved before stepping outside to catch his bus home.

Sharon's feelings haven't changed. "I do still believe. I believe that the seeds of love sown that year will some-day bring forth fruit in his life. Joey was worth it."

She also believes that God gave her a precious gift that school year—a glimpse of her sacred role as teacher.

The Sign

You will go out in joy and be led forth in peace;
the mountains and hills will burst into song before you,
and all the trees of the field will clap their hands.

—ISAIAH 55:12

Val headed north in the direction of her home-
town. The sun shimmered across a cloudless blue
sky that June afternoon, creating the impression
that all of nature was singing God's praises. Her
two "precious bundles" were asleep in back, and her
husband had drifted off to sleep in the passenger
seat up front. Val treasured that rare block of quiet
time. It allowed her mind to revisit the events of the
past year.

The year had introduced drastic changes into her life.
"I called it my roller-coaster year, because I had lived

through incredible highs and equally incredible lows," says Val.

Her faith had undergone repeated testing, and she'd slipped into a deep sense of despair. The year before, health issues had required her to undergo a complete hysterectomy. Her doctor had suspected ovarian cancer. For several weeks prior to her surgery, she pondered the details of her life. "I thought seriously about the direction I wanted to take, should God spare me from cancer," she says.

Val struggled with the real possibility that she might never be able to bear children. It had taken her a long time to realize how much she actually wanted to be a mother, only

> THE YEAR HAD INTRODUCED DRASTIC CHANGES INTO HER LIFE.

now to lose that dream. She also experienced moments when she questioned God's very existence.

During moments of doubt she would bargain with God, asking him to show her a tangible sign that he really cared. God chose to answer in a different way than she anticipated. "He didn't send a lightning bolt or other tangible signs that would boost my faith and give me hope." Instead, God had a better plan. He would send Val subtle reminders of his sweet presence.

Those reminders usually involved a personal, human touch of some sort—her husband's patience and understanding as she struggled with physical illness and spiritual doubt; the gracious care she received from doctors, friends, and family members; and the mysterious turn of events that catapulted her from a dark pit of despair into God's peaceful light.

"I had given up hope of ever having a baby, due to my infertility," explained Val. "But just when I was experiencing my darkest hour, another young woman was experiencing a similar despair." In a manner that only God could have orchestrated, two paths crossed. God's grace waited at the intersection, providing the answer to the cry of Val's heart.

"My daughter-to-be was born on the first day of spring," says Val.

She was a gift not only to Val and her husband, but also to Val's elderly father, who had long hoped for his "baby" to have one of her own. "My father also wanted to live to be eighty. He accomplished both goals that season."

Val's last phone conversation with her dad ended with him singing a favorite song. It was a song he used to sing to her when she was a toddler. "His voice sounded weak and faltering, and I could tell he was crying," says Val. "He sang to me as well as to our own little girl who lay in my arms."

Val sang along too, and their conversation ended with "I love you."

The day before her thirty-fourth birthday, her dad passed away. Val's joy came to a screeching halt, but she remembers turning to God with her sorrow. "I had faith and conviction that the Lord would cushion my crash, and I was able to truly believe that Dad had met his Lord and Savior."

Val marvels at how her life came full circle that year. And through it all—the surgery, the emotional turmoil, the joyous birth of her daughter, and the death of her father—the Lord never budged an inch. He was right there beside her, offering comfort, strength, and love. He listened to the cry of her heart when she felt angry or doubtful. He soothed her despair as a father would comfort his daughter. He wept when she wept—and rejoiced when she learned to lean fully on him again.

> GOD SOOTHED HER DESPAIR AS A FATHER WOULD COMFORT HIS DAUGHTER.

Val's thoughts returned to the road ahead and she whispered, "I love you, Lord." At that moment, she happened to glance up at an overpass, where someone had painted a message in bright red letters: "I love you, Valerie!"

Coincidence? Val doesn't think so.

TWENTY-SIX

High Tide

Our Adversary majors in three things:
noise, hurry, and crowds. If he can keep us engaged in
"muchness" and "manyness," he will rest satisfied.

—RICHARD J. FOSTER

When Becky walks along a beach, she doesn't like stopping to chat with other walkers. She'd much rather keep moving and spend her time focusing on God's beautiful creation. "It's a special time for me, and I enjoy feeling a personal communion with him, free from human interruptions," she says.

Becky recalls one summer in particular—the last before her family moved to Virginia—when she took long walks at Pawleys Island, South Carolina. Long, lazy days invited such outings, and mornings began early as runners, walkers, and cyclists headed to the sandy shore.

Certain early risers came seeking solitude, like Becky, while others stopped to socialize along the way. Becky admits to being irritated by these chatty intrusions, but adds, "I realized I was feeling like Scrooge, so I tried not to let the well-wishers get to me."

On her final morning walk, she was happy to find her usual route practically deserted. At last, she felt fully alone with God—pure bliss! The first half of her trek took her along a street heading south. Midway through her journey, she crossed over the dunes by way of a wooden plank walkway, on a sandy return route to her cottage. This was her routine every day. At the crest of the walkway, she paused to bask in a sunny spot before turning north.

But she was met with a surprise—high tide! Her usual wide route of white sand was now a sea of frothy surf, leaving her with barely enough room to walk. Frustrated by the sudden change, she had little choice but to welcome the challenge. "The roar of the surf was mesmerizing," says Becky. "Its expanse was breathtaking. I couldn't turn away."

CERTAIN EARLY RISERS CAME SEEKING SOLITUDE, LIKE BECKY, WHILE OTHERS STOPPED TO SOCIALIZE ALONG THE WAY.

Reveling in the new adventure, she trudged through deep, loose sand, staying closer to the dunes than usual. The break in her daily routine felt good. Even more exciting was the fact that the entire beach was empty. It was a first, and she describes it as a dream come true—a welcoming path, the ocean rushing in to meet her, and God by her side. "The feeling of oneness with God was as undeniable as the taste of salty spray and the sound of waves lapping at my feet."

ON THE PATH AHEAD, FOOTPRINTS HAD LEFT EVIDENCE OF A STRONG, INTENTIONAL STRIDE.

A curious sight slowed her pace. On the path ahead, footprints had left evidence of a strong, intentional stride. Funny, she hadn't noticed anyone else ahead of her on the long stretch of beach. The footprints were headed in the same direction she was walking, but appeared much bigger than hers.

Becky thought of the well-known poem "Footprints in the Sand," which describes how God carries us through the trials of life. But she sensed that God was using this set of prints to teach her something different.

"The trail through the sand made me think about some confusing steps I was about to take in my life. My husband and I had made plans to move from South Carolina to Virginia. Neither of us had jobs yet. We hadn't sold our house, and we were thousands of dollars in debt. We would be moving in with family soon so our kids could begin the school year on time."

This would be their fourth move in eight years, and Becky felt anxious about whether they were making the right decision.

As she walked along, dodging the lapping water, the Lord reminded her of a familiar passage of Scripture that assures us of God's loving provision: "Trust in the Lord with all your heart and lean not on your own understanding; in all your ways acknowledge him, and he will make your paths straight" (Proverbs 3:5, 6).

Could it be that God has already straightened my path, but I don't recognize or understand it yet? wondered Becky.

"The high tide gave me the chance to see my own life's path more clearly. So little sand was exposed, I was forced to limit my steps to that one narrow stretch of sand, rather than wandering all over the beach as usual."

Best of all, God had granted her heart's desire—a time of solitude so she could walk and think without distraction.

> BECKY BELIEVES GOD LEFT THE FOOTPRINTS IN THE SAND AS A SIGN ESPECIALLY FOR HER.

Becky believes God left the footprints in the sand as a sign especially for her. She was to leave her usual route and trust him—to follow without hesitation, just as she was following the prints along that narrow stretch of beach.

God was assuring her that he had already gone before, smoothing the path and preparing the way. She could entrust her future completely to him.

High tide may have interrupted her carefully laid plans, but it also delivered an unforgettable gift that day—a fresh glimpse of God.

Corrected by Love

The mother's heart is the child's schoolroom.

—HENRY WARD BEECHER

Parenting is filled with surprises, and one thing is sure: each child is unique.

"My first daughter was a breeze," says Sarah. "Her desire to please made for mostly pain-free toddler years. She loathed getting in trouble, so most of the time she simply obeyed. Corrections were met with true sorrow and rarely had to be repeated."

Then along came daughter number two. Cassie was a beautiful little girl with blond curls that framed her face and her big expressive eyes. From the beginning, she possessed a strong will and easily found ways to push her mom to the limit.

"Every time I turned around, I felt like I was correcting her."

Cassie drew on the walls with markers. She teased and chased the cats until they retaliated. And she was the one who would stubbornly refuse to do what she was told.

> SHE BEGAN TO WONDER WHY SHE WASN'T ABLE TO DISCIPLINE HER CHILD WITHOUT FEELING HEARTBROKEN.

One Sunday, Sarah remembers feeling at the end of her rope with Cassie. "I was sitting in the foyer of our church with the glazed look of defeat plastered on my face."

An older, wiser mom noticed her expression and asked what was troubling her. Sarah responded by bursting into tears, and she poured her heart out about Cassie. "She just doesn't listen. I feel like a horrible mother because all I've done is spank her this week."

"It will get better," the woman, named Terri, said. "I promise. My second daughter was the same way and she's become a delightful young woman. Just be consistent and it will bear good fruit."

Her words felt like a comforting salve and convinced Sarah that she was doing the right thing by disciplining her daughter. Someday, the daily wrestling with three-year-old Cassie would bear good fruit. These difficult years would not be wasted.

Sarah also realized that their ongoing struggles weren't

going to disappear overnight. "Every time Cassie got in trouble, the tears flowed and she let out howls that ripped straight through me. I hated scolding her and spanking her because it made me feel like the Wicked Witch of the West."

She began to wonder why she wasn't able to discipline her child without feeling heartbroken. "One afternoon, soon after my meltdown at church, Cassie was having a particularly difficult day. That naturally meant that I was having a dreadful day. She was crying and yelling after being scolded for yet another infraction that I now can't even recall."

She plopped Cassie into the time-out chair in an exasperated attempt to delay another scolding. Cassie's eyes begged her mother not to spank her, and Sarah could hardly take another round. "I wondered why this part of my life—Mom as discipliner—had so knotted up my heart."

Then God spoke to her in a simple statement. It wasn't a question or a directive, just an observation from a Father who knew her well: *You want her to like you.*

Sarah remembers the effect of those six little words and says they stopped her in her tracks. At that moment she realized that she hated disciplining her child because she was more worried about Cassie not liking her than she was about dealing with her daughter's disobedient heart. The realization came to Sarah's mind suddenly, like sunlight shining through a just-opened window blind—she had been giving in to every insecurity and memory of rejection in her own life, instead of trusting God to enable her to love Cassie in a way that isn't always easy.

That single crystal-clear moment transformed her as a parent. Sarah explains, "It was so easy to take Cassie's anger or rejection personally, instead of focusing on my job as her mom. Those simple words from the Lord reminded me that I had an important job to do, and my torment over doing it was not about her—it was about my own fears and insecurity."

SARAH IS NOW ABLE TO TAKE A DEEP BREATH AND REMEMBER IT'S NOT ABOUT HER, BUT ABOUT GOD'S PLAN FOR THE FUTURE.

Sarah scooped Cassie up in her arms and kissed her, smoothing her curls. "I loved this child, and loving her meant that I needed to help her rather than protect myself. Everything changed for me that day."

Sarah is now able to take a deep breath and remember it's not about her, but about God's plan for the future. "I remind myself that it's OK if my kids get mad at me or cry. It's fine if I lose my status as favorite parent. I do what needs to be done."

TWENTY-EIGHT

Crushed Like the Crocus

God sweetens outward pain with inward peace.

—THOMAS WATSON

A friend had given Marion's mother a dish of beautiful crocuses. Marion promised to plant them where her mother could enjoy them from the window of her apartment. Little did she know that she'd be planting them at the cemetery instead.

The following spring, Marion visited her mother's grave and discovered the groundskeeper had run his lawn mower over the transplanted crocuses. One glance at the flattened plants left Marion thinking, *I feel just like that—mowed down.*

The past year had proven to be one of the most difficult

years of her life. Two days after a big family reunion, Marion's mother suffered a severe asthma attack that took her life. As the oldest child, Marion felt a responsibility to sift through decades of belongings that had accumulated in her mother's apartment. Deciding what to keep, what to give away, and what to toss out was an enormous job. Everything had to go.

Marion invited the grandchildren to choose keepsakes from Grandma's apartment. Her aunts—sisters of her mother—each claimed a family heirloom.

"We children took what we wanted, but our houses were small, with not much space to store anything other than memories," said Marion. Her brother loaded his truck with items without much thought as to whether he could use them or not. Another relative showed up—one the family rarely saw. Marion kept quiet and stood aside as the woman pawed through her mother's belongings. She left with a load and returned later for more. Marion fumed. *What right does she have to my mother's things?*

By the end of July, Marion had emptied and thoroughly cleaned the apartment. It was time to go. With a heavy heart, she closed and locked the door behind her for the last time. The place was ready to be rented to a new tenant.

As caretaker of her mother's car, Marion agreed that once the estate settled, she would turn the car over to her niece, who drove a dilapidated car that was running on borrowed time. Grandma's car seemed like a perfect solution to her dilemma.

"My brother called impatiently several times, asking when his daughter could have the car," says Marion. During their conversations, though, he admitted that she really just planned to sell both her old car and her grandmother's car to fund a newer, flashier car for herself.

Marion was stunned by the news. It seemed to her that no one cared about her mother's things or what they meant to her. Resentment that had been building up in her since her mother's death took hold of her heart. "Meanwhile, my neighbor had looked over the car and noted all the work that needed to be done on it," she recounts. Thinking that she was saving her niece a lot of expense and trouble to make the car ready for sale, Marion sold the car to the guy next door. She divided the money between her three siblings and herself.

> AFTER THE STRESS OF THE PAST SEVERAL MONTHS, SHE DESPERATELY NEEDED THAT WEEK TO RELAX AND ENJOY THE SEA BREEZES IN MAINE.

Her mother's estate settled right before Marion's planned vacation in September. After the stress of the past several months, she desperately needed that week to relax and enjoy the sea breezes in Maine. But shortly after arriving at her motel, she received a phone call from another brother, who said he had bad news. Marion's niece had been killed in a terrible car wreck. Her father had been driving, and he was seriously injured.

Marion's thoughts raced as the news sank in. Had she done the right thing by selling her mother's car to her neighbor instead of giving it to her niece? If she had gone ahead and given it to her, maybe she would have been driving it instead of riding with her father that fateful night.

Now, standing at her mother's grave, tears flowed freely. "I missed my mother, but I knew she was no longer suffering. I thought about my niece, who had died at such a young age, leaving a two-year-old daughter. I thought, too, about my brother, who was still recuperating from the accident, and whose life would never be the same."

GOD INTERVENED AND SPOKE SOOTHING WORDS TO MARION'S GRIEVING HEART.

God intervened and spoke soothing words to Marion's grieving heart. He assured her that the accident was not her fault. He also pointed out the deep-seated resentment that had taken root in her heart. Silently, she prayed for forgiveness and asked the Lord to replace bitterness with love. When it was time to leave, she felt at peace with both the Lord and her family.

"When I turned the key in the ignition," says Marion, "the radio came on with a song I'd never heard before. I'll always remember those comforting words: 'Your

Father understands, he knows what you're going through . . .'"

Hope flooded over her. Her life would indeed bloom again—just like the mowed-down crocuses at her mother's grave.

NINE

Seven Little Words

We are always on the anvil;
by trials God is shaping us for higher things.
—Henry Ward Beecher

"I didn't want to be a mother," says Glenda. Seven little words—but it was the truth.

"My temper would never make it through all those years of raising children. While I didn't show it on the outside, I was a boiling volcano inside. The only thing that kept me from erupting was that I tried to create an outward impression that I was calm, ladylike, and in control."

During her childhood years, Glenda had tried to picture what it would feel like to be a grown-up. Filled with anger, she figured adulthood would mean having the freedom to tear things apart and destroy whatever she desired. She'd be able to release her anger whenever and however.

"I never told anyone how I felt inside. Most of the time I took it out on my imaginary playmate. I knew people would think I was crazy if they could read my thoughts. I knew those thoughts weren't right."

When she entered college, she felt a sense of control. "I'd heard so much yelling and fighting between my parents, living on my own was like living in paradise."

Shortly before her senior year in college, Glenda married a wonderful, loving man. Jack has proved to be an ideal husband, who helped her find a balance she'd never experienced before. Almost six years into their marriage, she became pregnant. She decided to share the news with Jack over dinner at their favorite restaurant. "I slipped a tiny gold package onto his plate. Because we often surprised each other, the present was nothing unusual—until he opened it."

> DURING HER CHILDHOOD YEARS, GLENDA HAD TRIED TO PICTURE WHAT IT WOULD FEEL LIKE TO BE A GROWN-UP.

Glenda recalls every detail of that evening. Jack's eyes widened as he shifted his gaze from the opened box to Glenda and back again. It was obvious that he realized the significance of the gift. When he held up the tiny pair of booties for inspection, Glenda nodded her head up and down in a wordless affirmation.

"I loved being pregnant," she says. "We made plans as I embroidered a baby blanket. My worries about becoming a mother were over—at least until the day Dave was born."

During the ride to the hospital, every fear rose to the surface. Glenda panicked and thought, *What if we've made the wrong decision to have kids?*

GLENDA PANICKED AND THOUGHT, *WHAT IF WE'VE MADE THE WRONG DECISION TO HAVE KIDS?*

With Jack's perpetual good nature, he said, "Come on. Everything will be fine."

Glenda wasn't so sure. "My sense of apprehension was too powerful. Soon after the delivery, my usual temper was apparent. I knew inside me I had the capacity to physically and emotionally harm someone. My eyes had witnessed continual rage between my parents while I was growing up. Plus, when I was only in the sixth grade, I had a cousin who in a fit of rage killed his own wife. I knew firsthand what uncontrolled anger could do, and I knew I had that same emotion inside me."

Dave was about four months old, dressed in soft, clean jammies, snuggled in his crib with his feet tucked up under him—his favorite sleeping position. Glenda stood beside the crib, resting her hand across his arched back. The only sound came from a clock ticking away the fleeting moments.

Glenda cried out to God. She told him that she never wanted to harm her children. "Please help me be a good mother!" she prayed. Just seven little words, but God took them to heart.

She didn't notice a change at first. "Daily activities led from one day to the next," says Glenda, "but a couple of months later I started noticing that I didn't have the intense feeling of hatred I'd always had."

It seemed almost strange to feel the anger lifting. In fact, she was so hesitant about declaring it gone, she didn't want to talk about it yet. What if it returned? Two or three months lapsed without a single angry outburst. "It was as if I were standing outside my body and observing myself. I finally asked Jack, 'Have you noticed anything different about me? Do I seem like I get as angry as I used to?'"

> GOD WAS LISTENING TO MY PRAYER, AND HE TOOK MY RAGE AWAY.

Jack admitted he had noticed a definite difference. "You know, I sort of wondered about that, but didn't want to say anything because it's really been nice," he said. "You don't seem like the same person anymore."

Their "baby," Dave, is now thirty years old. Glenda admits to experiencing what she calls "little temper tantrums," now and then, but that vile temper that made her want to destroy things and hurt people has not resurfaced.

"It never returned," says Glenda. "God was listening to my prayer, and he took my rage away. He granted what I wanted most—to be a good mother."

THIRTY

Changing Direction

Praise be to the God and Father of our Lord Jesus Christ,
the Father of compassion and the God of all comfort, who comforts
us in all our troubles, so that we can comfort those in any
trouble with the comfort we ourselves have received from God.

—2 CORINTHIANS 1:3, 4

Being a nurse was a major part of Cherry's identity. "The work was stressful, but it was gratifying to know that I was making a difference in the lives of my patients." Even so, after almost twenty years in her vocation, Cherry felt restless. "The excitement and joy was fading, and I dreaded going back to work after my days off."

One day while driving to work, she gripped the steering wheel and cried out to God. Pouring out deep-seated frustrations, she laid her future out for him to examine. "Lord," she prayed, "I'm not happy with my job anymore, but I can't leave because the money's too good. Besides, what else would I do? Where do you want me to go from here, Lord? If you want me to do something else, please show me. You might have to shout at me, because you know I don't always want to hear advice."

CHERRY WORRIED CONSTANTLY THAT ONE MINOR ERROR MIGHT TURN OUT TO BE THE ONE THAT COULD CAUSE HARM TO A PATIENT.

A few months later, Cherry began to develop symptoms of obsessive-compulsive disorder (OCD), which made it difficult for her to continue working as a home health nurse. "In my mind, I began to magnify the mistakes of my fellow home health nurses and became increasingly afraid that I would make mistakes too. I felt like a policeman or a repairman as I went on my rounds, catching errors and problems, saving my patients from certain danger."

Cherry worried constantly that one minor error might turn out to be the one that could cause harm to a patient. She spent her days off and most evenings mentally reviewing patients under her care. The job that had once fulfilled her was now a source of dread. She felt tortured by fear and worry.

"When other nurses started complaining about my super vigilance, and patients became alarmed by my attention to insignificant symptoms, I sought help," says Cherry. That is when she was diagnosed with obsessive-compulsive disorder. Her supervisor was supportive throughout her recovery and reduced her workload to allow her to work fewer days per week. But the truth was, she battled a constant urge to give in to the obsessive thoughts and compulsive behaviors.

Cherry recalled the day she'd cried out to God. Was OCD a tool that God was using to point her life in a new direction? She began to ponder how she might combine her nursing skills with a long-buried passion for writing in order to reach out to others suffering with OCD.

Since her family would no longer benefit from a second paycheck, Cherry included them all in her decision-making process. "We prayed together about it and decided I would take a year off work. At the end of that first year, we'd decide if God was indeed calling me to be a writer."

The Lord opened opportunities for her to share her journey with OCD. "I wrote an article about my experience for a Christian nursing magazine, followed by more articles and a continuing education home-study course for nurses."

Then, through a series of remarkable events, Cherry coauthored seven books within eight years for a group of psychologists. The books were aimed at the secular book market, but she wrote them in a manner that was acceptable to a Christian readership as well. Her teenage son also helped create a Web site that would reach out to Christians challenged by the struggles of OCD.

Cherry recalls times of serious doubt. "In the midst of my struggle with OCD, I had trouble seeing God's plan for my life. Why would he allow this illness to threaten my nursing career? I took great pride in being a nurse, so much that I failed to realize that God could use me in any other way. My identity was wrapped up in nursing clothes rather than in the blood of Christ."

> IN THE MIDST OF MY STRUGGLE WITH OCD, I HAD TROUBLE SEEING GOD'S PLAN FOR MY LIFE.

Years later, she realizes that in order for God to redirect a life, one must reach a point of brokenness. God has a reason for any illness he allows into our lives, but he never leaves us to fend for ourselves. "Through all the dark days, I found comfort in the Word," reveals Cherry. "When the days brightened, with the comfort I had received I was able to minister online to people with OCD."

God not only provided Cherry with a new identity as a writer; he drew her closer to himself, where she had belonged all along.

THIRTY-ONE

Right on Time

"For I know the plans I have for you,"
declares the Lord, "plans to prosper you and not to harm you,
plans to give you hope and a future."

—JEREMIAH 29:11

If someone had asked James where he would end up after his college graduation, he would never have predicted the life he leads today. After earning a degree in journalism, he wound up working in public relations for a Christian college. Nine years later, he continued his studies in marketing communications and landed a job in journalism.

After marrying Shannon, a lot more surprises were in store. Four months into their marriage, for example, he had the privilege of breaking an important piece of news to her—they were expecting a baby. Barely settled into a two-bedroom apartment near Chicago, they both led busy lives with little time left over. Shannon was studying hard to complete her last semester of nursing school while working as a unit secretary at the hospital. By that point, James had been a journalist for almost four years, and a couple of weeks earlier, they'd bought their first new car together.

Life was good, but very full. Children were definitely not in the picture until the couple felt more settled and secure. Shannon would graduate and find a nursing job, they'd buy a house, and someday they'd consider starting a family. But not yet.

SHANNON WOULD GRADUATE AND FIND A NURSING JOB, THEY'D BUY A HOUSE, AND SOMEDAY THEY'D CONSIDER STARTING A FAMILY.

They'd had one pregnancy scare just recently, which turned out to be a false alarm. "However, the Lord must have had other ideas," says James.

Shannon was scheduled for an evening shift while James was working his normal eight to five. After work, as was his habit, he grabbed the mail from the mailbox and then took the stairs to their apartment to check the answering machine.

The first message was from Shannon's doctor. "I'm sorry for the mix-up," he said, "but the other lab results were wrong. You are definitely pregnant."

Their entire life was about to change. Shannon would arrive home in two hours. How could he tell her?

In his brief period as a husband, he'd learned that a clean apartment makes for a happy wife. So his first thought was to do anything he could to help straighten things. "Never before or since have I cleaned like I cleaned that night," he says.

As zero hour approached, James tried calling a couple of friends for advice on how to break the news. They offered prayer support, which he desperately needed at the moment, though he admits, "A script might have come in handy."

Shannon finally arrived home. James played a Steven Curtis Chapman song on the stereo—"I Will Be Here," which was sung at their wedding (and which would later be sung by James at their baby's dedication). It was time to share the big news. "I don't beat around the bush very well," tells James, "so I looked into her eyes and told her straight out that a message was waiting on the answering machine from her doctor. 'The results they gave you before were wrong.' I said. 'You are pregnant.'"

AS ZERO HOUR APPROACHED, JAMES TRIED CALLING A COUPLE OF FRIENDS FOR ADVICE ON HOW TO BREAK THE NEWS.

Shannon paused for a minute, then burst into tears. They hugged, then prayed together, asking God to help them adjust to the unexpected change. "Eventually we reached a point where we realized that if God was going to give us a child this early in our marriage, he would also help equip us for parenthood."

They were still in the honeymoon stage of marriage; four months earlier they'd both been single, not anticipating expanding into a family. "Besides losing my home office, we worked through how Shannon felt about having to postpone her nursing career for a while."

Josh arrived shortly after the couple's first anniversary, followed fourteen months later by Brian. Tim completed the family circle soon after their fourth anniversary.

"The Beatles once sang that life is something that happens while you're planning something else. And yet," adds James, "if I had to do it all over again, I wouldn't change a thing."

God knew all along when he would bless James and Shannon with children. "Had things gone the way Shannon and I had planned, we'd have been at least five years into our marriage before kids came along," James says. "As it turned out, my dad died just before our fifth anniversary. He got to enjoy his grandchildren, giving Josh rides on the lawn tractor, introducing Brian to the pet bunnies he raised in his backyard, and cuddling baby Timothy."

Because of God's perfect timing, Josh and Brian have memories of their grandfather.

James has decided that on his own, he's a pretty lousy planner. "God knows what he's doing a lot better than I do. He's proven it over the course of our lives."

He's right on time, every time.

His Clearest Call

*Always seek peace between your heart and God, but in
this world, always be careful to remain ever-restless, never satisfied,
and always abounding in the work of the Lord.*

—JIM ELLIOT

Shortly after committing her life, family, and future to God, Glenda joined Bible Study Fellowship (BSF) to learn more about the Bible. The group rotated houses every month, sharing lunch and fellowship after their Bible study. At one of their luncheons, they took turns describing a godly person who had affected their lives. Glenda wanted to share all about her Aunt Bea, who had recently passed away.

"I had written a little poem about her that was printed in the handout for her funeral. I brought that handout to the luncheon, but worried that I might burst into tears if I spoke up."

She did read the poem, and several ladies commented afterwards on how her words had touched their hearts. One woman named Linda was a professional Christian author and speaker. She mentioned an upcoming Forest Home Writer's Conference that was going to be held about two hundred miles from Glenda's home in San Diego. "Linda had personal commitments, so she was unable to attend, but said she felt that the Lord wanted me to go," recalls Glenda. However, she was shocked to learn that the weeklong conference carried a price tag of three hundred dollars.

Glenda thanked Linda, but explained that not only was the conference too far away and too expensive, she had young children at home and didn't feel she could be away from them that long. At Linda's urging, she agreed to pray about it.

> GLENDA WANTED
> TO SHARE ALL ABOUT HER
> AUNT BEA, WHO HAD
> RECENTLY PASSED AWAY.

The next week at BSF, Linda asked Glenda whether she had sought God's direction about attending the conference. "Well, no, not really," admitted Glenda.

Linda was persistent. "Will you promise to pray about it before you say no?"

"OK, I will pray about it but . . ."

"No buts."

After BSF, as Glenda was driving to her dad's real estate office, she had a talk with God. "OK, Lord, I know it seems impossible and I'm not even sure I want to go, but if you want me to go to this writer's conference, you'll have to open all the doors."

An agent named Mary greeted her at the office, then asked, "Glenda, are you going to the Forest Home Christian Writer's Conference?"

The timing of Mary's question stunned Glenda. "Why are you asking me a question like that?"

"My husband is going, and he likes company when he drives."

> OK, LORD, I KNOW IT SEEMS IMPOSSIBLE AND I'M NOT EVEN SURE I WANT TO GO, BUT IF YOU WANT ME TO GO TO THIS WRITER'S CONFERENCE, YOU'LL HAVE TO OPEN ALL THE DOORS.

In a matter of minutes, God had provided transportation to the writer's conference if she wanted to go! Although surprised by the news, Glenda still had to consider the cost of attending, plus the week she would have to be away from her family.

She phoned her husband, Dick, and explained what had happened, then ended their conversation by wondering aloud how she could possibly be away a whole week. "Besides, we don't have three hundred dollars."

Dick didn't miss a beat. "We're getting three hundred dollars back from our income tax refund—and I want you to spend it to go to this writer's thing."

"But what about the kids?"

"No problem," he said. "I'll take them to school, and we can get a babysitter for a couple of hours each day until I get home from work."

Glenda attended the conference and roomed with a group of wonderful Christian women. During the week, God revealed ways in which he had led her to that point. "As we prayed, worshiped, and listened to speakers, it was like God was pointing directly at me, whispering, 'You are mine and this is the job I have for you.'"

On their final day together, conferees received an assignment: In one sentence, write how God has changed your life in a fresh and creative way.

Glenda wrote, "God shattered my plate-glass life; then he gathered up the broken pieces and made them into wind chimes."

God took that line and used it to confirm his plan for her—she was to use her gifts and abilities as a writer. In the years following the conference, that single line of text appeared in a variety of publications, from *Decision* magazine to the back cover of a book of inspirational poetry. The Lord created opportunities for her to attend more writer's conferences, where she connected with others who also published her work.

"One of the biggest surprises is that my niche turned out to be children's picture books. I have published sixteen books with five different Christian publishers," says Glenda. She now also teaches a children's writing course through the Institute of Children's Literature.

> THE LORD CREATED OPPORTUNITIES FOR HER TO ATTEND MORE WRITER'S CONFERENCES, WHERE SHE CONNECTED WITH OTHERS WHO ALSO PUBLISHED HER WORK.

Glenda's experience taught her the truth of Proverbs 3:5, 6: "Trust in the Lord with all your heart and lean not on your own understanding; in all your ways acknowledge him, and he will make your paths straight."

THIRTY-THREE

Sorrowful Surrender

Come to me, all you who are weary and burdened,
and I will give you rest.

—MATTHEW 11:28

"God, please help me! I feel dead inside," Jan had whispered to no one in particular. She was sitting at her kitchen table shortly after burying Chris, her only child.

Never would she forget that moment when a state trooper knocked on her door.

He was hyperventilating. *Perhaps this man is sick and needs help,* thought Jan.

"Are you Chris's mother?"

Her husband, Bill, had replied, "I'm his dad, and this is my wife, Jan."

"May I come in?" asked the trooper.

Jan remembers her knees shaking. "I didn't know whether to run, vomit, or hide."

"There's been a terrible wreck. We found a body. Is this your son's wallet?"

Later, the trooper would hand-deliver his report, detailing the wreck. "Chris sustained a broken neck and numerous other injuries. The drunk driver walked away unharmed," Jan recalls.

Friends and family gathered in Jan's home after the funeral. Chris's room at the corner of their rambling, ranch-style home looked exactly as he'd left it. "After the tragic news of his death, I wandered about his room, touching his horse show trophies, saddle, and treasured guitar. I embraced his pillow, smelling his scent, hoping this was a bad dream and not reality," says Jan.

Jan felt detached from the conversations that filled her home. Many of them centered around her emotional state.

"Did they arrest the drunk driver?" a neighbor asked.

"Yes, he's been arrested, but that won't bring Chris back," replied Jan's brother.

"She's survived terrible storms in the past, but I don't know about this one," observed a friend.

"Is she responding to anyone?" another family member asked in a hushed tone.

The words sounded a thousand miles away. Jan felt too distant to comprehend or respond, sinking deeper into her personal prison. "I pinched my arm with all my might and could feel no pain. No physical pain; no spiritual pulse either. I sensed I was slipping away."

> BEFORE CHRIS DIED, SHE HAD WRESTLED WITH PAST HURTS AND LOSSES, WHICH INCLUDED HORRIFIC CHILDHOOD ABUSE.

Before Chris died, she had wrestled with past hurts and losses, which included horrific childhood abuse. Doubt and shame had led her to turn her back on her faith. By allowing those experiences to overshadow the person God intended her to become, she had felt unlovable and unworthy. "I allowed my circumstances to control me, rather than surrendering my wounded heart to God," admits Jan.

Filled with fear and helplessness, she heard a voice speak to her; not audibly, but through her mind: *Do not fear. Be still, my daughter. I have your heart in mine; I am breathing life into you—be very still, my lost and broken lamb.*

When she lost Chris, Jan found it difficult to pray.

"The best I could do was groan and cry. God gave me the strength to put on my shoes every morning. He gave me the power to make it through each day, carrying me every step of the way."

Roger Nelson, the compassionate pastor who led Chris's funeral, stayed in touch with Jan and Bill in a kind and gentle way. One day, Roger asked if he could pray with them.

Jan won't ever forget his words. "Roger held Bill's hand and mine as he prayed, 'Father, you know the pain of losing a child. Your Son was killed, not by a drunk driver, but by men filled with hate and rage. God, I ask you to comfort Bill and Jan as they mourn the loss of Chris. We know in your timing, you will lead them to receive the loving support of others who also knew and loved Chris . . .'"

JAN WAS HUMBLED BY THE KINDNESS AND LOVE OF THIS WARM CHURCH FAMILY.

Shortly before Christmas, they entered Roger's church, the same church where Chris had been baptized at age ten, and where he had attended regularly with his grandpa. "People we didn't know walked up to us with hugs and kind words," Jan recalls.

"I loved Chris too," said an elderly lady.

"I miss Chris and pray for you every day," whispered a young boy.

"We have prayed that you would allow us to hold your hand," said a couple.

Jan was humbled by the kindness and love of this warm church family. When it came time for the service to begin, Roger commented about the beautiful Christmas tree located next to the piano.

"Our church purchased this reusable tree to honor the memory of Chris," Roger said.

Jan glanced at the wooden cross on top of the tree and silently prayed, *God, thank you for delivering me to this church today. I didn't want to come. I don't want to be around people. But I think I am supposed to be here.*

In their new journey, Jan and Bill sought to know God better. "I now realize that regardless of the storm, sorrow brings surrender. And surrender brings hope in Christ Jesus, who invites us to rest in him."

THIRTY-FOUR

Faith Like That

Faith is like radar that sees through the fog.

—CORRIE TEN BOOM

Mary is a woman whose faith has been stretched by a growing, daily dependence on God. Faith-filled believers from the past, such as George Mueller, have inspired her to set aside doubt and lean hard on the Lord.

"Mueller is known as the apostle of faith of the nine-teenth century," says Mary. "He established orphanages and then supported them without telling anyone of his needs. He simply prayed and trusted God to provide."

Mary recalls reading about one orphanage that had run out of food. Their dilemma didn't seem to worry Mueller at all. "The table was set, everyone was seated, and Mr. Mueller thanked the Lord for his provision."

Mueller finished his prayer moments before someone knocked on the door. A bread wagon had broken down in front of the orphanage. The driver was in a hurry and needed to get rid of the bread. "Could the orphanage use any bread?" he wondered. Mary imagined the squeals of the children as the Lord blessed them with fresh bread, hand-delivered to the door, no less.

A short while later, someone else arrived unexpectedly, with enough milk for all the children. "They had a feast directly from the hand of God," recounts Mary.

As a single mother of three, Mary craved a deep, abiding faith like George Mueller's. She became determined to follow his example of praying and waiting on the Lord. Sharing her specific financial needs with God alone, she decided to enroll in college. She had no idea how it would all work out financially, because her entire income every week went to caring for her children.

> AS A SINGLE MOTHER OF THREE, MARY CRAVED A DEEP, ABIDING FAITH LIKE GEORGE MUELLER'S.

One day, she sat with a group of young students, eating her brown-bag lunch. She told them how God had promised to supply her needs, right down to practical, daily expenses like bus fare and milk money. But Mary was concerned about how the faith of her younger friends might be affected if God's timing didn't agree with hers.

One day she didn't even have milk money, so she spent her study hour pleading with God to provide what she needed. On the way to the cafeteria, she ran into Laura, who asked, "Mary, would you be offended if I loaned you five dollars?"

> GOD USED A FRIEND'S GENEROSITY AS AN OPPORTUNITY TO TEACH THEM BOTH A LESSON ABOUT GIVING AND RECEIVING.

"Well, I don't know when I could pay it back."

Laura shrugged. "It doesn't matter." She stuffed the money into Mary's hand.

The next day, Laura apologized for offering the money as a loan and said she didn't want the money returned. God used a friend's generosity as an opportunity to teach them both a lesson about giving and receiving.

Mary's prayer life grew stronger as God filled in every gap. One Friday on her way home from class, she realized that she had only one bus token left for the next day's fare. She didn't have money to buy another token. Worry crept up on her, but God immediately reminded her of George Mueller's daily faith walk.

She remembered a Bible verse that promises, "Before they call I will answer; while they are still speaking I will hear" (Isaiah 65:24). God showed her firsthand what the verse meant.

That Friday at home, Mary found a message on her answering machine. A doctor's office had heard she was available for work, and offered her a job for the very next day. She would need her last bus token to ride to work.

Her mind raced ahead. *How will I get home if he doesn't pay me at the end of the day? How will I get to school on Monday without a token?*

"I did go to work," says Mary, "but the doctor did not mention paying me that day. I straightened up the desk and was heading for the door when he called after me, 'Mary, I forgot my checkbook this morning. Go ahead and take your pay for today out of the petty cash drawer.'"

Last-minute answers were often nerve-racking, but God's timing was never too early or too late. Mary learned to relax and to wait for him to work things out.

In the following years, God provided countless opportunities to wait on him. Mary compares her experience to that of the Israelites in the wilderness. When the Israelites were to cross the Jordan into the promised land, the priests physically had to step out and dip their toes into the water before the waters opened. Mary figures her daily dependence on God was like that. Step by step, God led her into a deeper walk—a journey of faith that would carry her through anything life tossed her way.

"It is easier now to have faith in the bigger things because of God's faithfulness in those first steps of learning to trust him."

Lesson of the Button

Faith makes all things possible. Love makes all things easy.

—Dwight L. Moody

When Jennifer was young, she received an award for perfect attendance at Summer Vacation Bible Camp—a cute button with a cartoon frog and words that read, "Who you are is your gift from God. What you make of yourself is your gift to God."

She hung the button on the end of a light cord in her closet, and there it stayed throughout her childhood. Each time she turned the light off or on, she'd touch that button. "Despite my familiarity with it, it was only many, many years later, after an emergency C-section, that I came to understand what the button really meant," says Jennifer.

Her second pregnancy had ended seven weeks early with the birth of fraternal twins. At five days old, one of the babies, Avery, was diagnosed with Down syndrome. Both babies remained in the NICU, and Jennifer traveled seventy-five miles each day to be able to hold them for one hour each visit.

After returning home every afternoon, Jennifer would stroll down a wooded path, where the air smelled smoky from distant forest fires. The path ended at a lake below her house, where mountains, like big-shouldered brothers on every side, protected the water. That daily ritual felt as necessary as the air she breathed.

"I'd carefully cross the grassy slope that led to the gravel beach, its cool smooth stones all the colors of the earth—ochre and gray, blue, brown, green, and black. I'd wade in until the water reached my knees," says Jennifer. "Then I'd kneel down into it, letting the current carry me away from shore. I'd spread my arms wide, suspended, held there by surface tension, and by my resistance to gravity, by life and breath and air, the difference between floating and drowning just a matter of inches."

> HER SECOND PREGNANCY HAD ENDED SEVEN WEEKS EARLY WITH THE BIRTH OF FRATERNAL TWINS.

The water was cold and clear—glacial runoff that had once sat at the peaks of the surrounding mountains. "For the first time all day, I would begin to shake, not from a chill but from a grief so deep, I couldn't find the tears," says Jennifer.

She wrestled with a choice that had to be made. "I could be a person who fell apart, a person who stopped trying, a person who felt overwhelmed and quit. Or I could choose another way. I was so full of doubt, anger, and guilt. It was the hardest time of my life, and even as I was struggling with it, somewhere deep in my subconscious lived the lesson of the button."

When Jennifer thinks back to that time now, she is reminded of hands—"hands working for us, some belonging to people I'd known for years, like my parents, or my husband's, or my friends Phyllis, Sarah, Emily, and Carrie. Other helping hands belonged to strangers— nurses whose names I could barely keep straight, social workers, doctors, and neighbors I knew just by sight."

She remembers hands folded in prayer, hands lifting baby clothes fresh out of the dryer and folding them into boxes for her, and hands dialing phone numbers as their news spread.

"A woman whose name I will never know helped me find my car when I was sobbing so hard I couldn't see straight. Another person offered the phone number of her sister, who had a child with Down syndrome."

She recalls hands gently holding hers, hands helping her up when she felt unable to help herself. Wherever she went, she felt cradled and loved.

Before the tiniest of smiles, before the blink of an eyelash, before the first sweet breath, two tiny heartbeats echoed just beneath Jennifer's rib cage, there below her own heart. "We started as three points of a triangle, close as could be, and though we have widened, we are a triangle still, connected no longer by blood and muscle and tissue but by one word—*family*."

Avery and his twin brother are now two. He has hair the color of wheat and eyes like a river. He charmingly teaches without realizing he is a teacher. "He eats pears with gleeful abandon, but when I hold up a green bean, he turns his head away in disdain," says Jennifer. "At our house, people take their shoes off and leave them in a line by the door. When no one is looking, Avery tucks things into the empty shoes, like parting gifts—a toy car, a tiny horse, a pilfered spoon . . ."

> HE IS THE CHILD THAT I WANTED, THAT I DID NOT KNOW I WANTED. HE IS MY SON.

Despite the stubbed toes, the lost spoons, and their startled guests, it's hard for her to be mad at him. "He is the child that I wanted, that I did not know I wanted. He is my son."

He is the fulfillment of the long-ago award, and the lesson she didn't know she would learn so well: "Who I am is my gift from God. What I make of myself is my gift to God."

THIRTY-SIX

Beyond the Windmill

The Lord is close to the brokenhearted
and saves those who are crushed in spirit.

—PSALM 34:18

A familiar musty smell stirred memories as I struggled down the cellar steps with my basket of dirty clothes," says Gay. "It reminded me of all those rainy days my siblings and I played down there when we were growing up."

In the corner of the cellar beside a washing machine stood her father's old work table. Scratched and scarred from years of use, the table now held loose wooden pieces of a model windmill project he'd begun. A thick layer of dust revealed how long it had been since he'd last worked on it.

Curiosity drew her in for a closer look, and she noticed

a faded drawing sitting next to the wooden pieces. "As I compared the drawing to the model, I could see several added-on details my father had incorporated. I picked up one of its arms and immediately spotted a mistake. He'd assembled the crosspieces backwards."

Gay heard heavy steps on the wooden spacers behind her as her father shuffled over to stand beside her. Motioning to his dusty project, he asked, "Well, what do you think?"

"It's really nice, Dad. There's not much left to do on it, is there?"

"Oh, one of these days I'll finish it." He told her how he wanted to add another step before the doorway to the wooden windmill, then admitted he hadn't quite figured out how to do it yet.

Gay knew exactly what the problem was, but didn't want to embarrass him by questioning his expertise. She could spot his error, but unfortunately, he wasn't able to think through the details of assembly. It was as though a lightbulb had gone out. He simply didn't understand.

In the corner of the cellar beside a washing machine stood her father's old work table.

It saddened Gay to see how the years had changed her dad. "Here was someone whose carpentry skills had once provided for a growing family of eight," says Gay. "One of his proudest achievements was the work he did on a full-size wooden model of the first nuclear submarine."

But like a magician waving a cruel wand, Alzheimer's disease had suddenly slowed his movements and destroyed his access to what he loved best. To those who knew and loved him, it seemed as though he had been robbed of everything enjoyable in life.

LIKE A MAGICIAN WAVING A CRUEL WAND, ALZHEIMER'S DISEASE HAD SUDDENLY SLOWED HIS MOVEMENTS AND DESTROYED HIS ACCESS TO WHAT HE LOVED BEST.

Simple repairs around the house turned into long, frustrating sessions, usually ending in his giving up in the middle of a task. The last time he visited Gay's home, she noticed how much the disease had ravaged him both physically and mentally. Before, she'd always saved him some sort of building project because he loved helping out whenever possible. This time she'd set aside built-in cabinets that she hoped he would be able to install along one wall of the back entry area.

Gay was preparing lunch and would pause every so often to watch him work. That's when she saw him stretch a tape measure across a space to see how long he should cut his board. He turned to the board and marked it, then measured the space again to double-check. "He repeated himself several times, and my heart ached as I realized what was happening," says Gay.

The insidious disease was now affecting his short-term memory. It made him question his accuracy just because his brain couldn't retain the necessary measurement long enough for him to trust that it was correct.

If he was having trouble remembering a simple measurement, Gay wondered how he could possibly handle driving the long distance back to Connecticut. She rode along as a passenger, which was nerve-racking. "At one point during our drive, we entered heavy city traffic that squeezed three lanes to two because of construction. Daddy's perception was that we were approaching a toll booth, so he began to dig around in his coin purse."

She watched with mounting horror as their vehicle drifted to within inches of the car beside them while he dug around for the correct change. God watched over them, and they somehow made it to Connecticut without a disaster. Gay had no choice but to take over the driving from that point on.

Gay's mind jerked back to the present, as her dad ran his fingers over the abandoned pieces of his wooden windmill. "Maybe I'll finish it one day," he repeated, "or maybe I won't."

IT TOOK EVERY OUNCE OF SELF-CONTROL TO KEEP FROM WRAPPING HER ARMS AROUND HIM IN PITY.

She sensed his resignation and watched him turn and walk away. Her eyes filled with tears. It took every ounce of self-control to keep from wrapping her arms around him in pity.

As much as she longed to comfort him, God helped her to give her dad what he needed most: the unconditional love of a daughter who realized his need for dignity.

How Sweet the Sound

Whatever enlarges hope will also exalt courage.

—SAMUEL JOHNSON

The summer before her freshman year in high school, Lucy learned to play a ukulele. "Not only was it fun, it was a lifesaver the day I took it to my English class. Since I had a problem speaking without a stutter, I was afraid that someone might laugh at me if I tried to read my poem." She came up with an ingenious idea. Instead of reciting her poem, she played her uke and sang the words to the tune of "Good Night, Irene," a popular song that year.

Singing took the focus off her stutter, and she was able to join her classmates as they laughed at her silly poem. But that was just one class, and Lucy knew that she couldn't sing her way through high school—or through life. *Why does my stutter disappear when I sing?* she wondered.

Lucy's mother looked for a way to help by reading books about stuttering. She learned that stuttering is often an emotional problem and may have nothing to do with a physical impairment. Lucy visited a psychiatrist friend of her family.

"I explained to Dr. Beckman that I loved my parents very much, but I could feel tension in our home. My father worked long hours as a builder and was usually tired and short-tempered. My mother was busy each day volunteering."

As the youngest child, Lucy often felt lonely. Her sister was nine years older and was considered both brilliant and beautiful. She received most of the family attention. "I remember wanting to be like her," says Lucy.

School only added to her stress, so after a few counseling sessions, Dr. Beckman suggested that she attend school away from home. A change of environment might help ease her stuttering.

Lucy remembers the discussion that followed. Her parents didn't want her to move alone, so they decided that her mother would move with her. In fact, they said that her mom's arthritis would benefit from a warmer climate—a kind way to try to help Lucy adjust. Mom and daughter left their home in South Carolina and moved to Fort Lauderdale, Florida. Old friends welcomed them into an apartment adjoining their home, and they had time to settle in before school began.

Lucy recalls feeling excited about starting over. Her teachers and classmates were friendly, and her environment was beautiful—beautiful white sand surrounding the buildings, and palm trees swaying in the breeze.

One day some girls at school invited her to visit their church on Sunday. God was providing everything she needed, including a group of new friends.

> GOD WAS PROVIDING EVERYTHING SHE NEEDED, INCLUDING A GROUP OF NEW FRIENDS.

In English class, book reports were due. "My English teacher, Mrs. Hendricks, was a gentle, caring woman. She expected me to report on a book of my choosing, but didn't know that I had a speech problem and a fear of standing before class," said Lucy.

Lucy was excited about the book she chose, and looked forward to sharing its message with her classmates. It wasn't until she finished that she realized she had not stuttered a single word!

After a carefree school year, her mother decided it was time to return to South Carolina. "My stuttering was gone, and the warmer climate had helped her arthritis," remembers Lucy.

Life was not to be that simple though. As soon as classes began in September, her stuttering returned.

Heartbroken, she returned to the high school in Ft. Lauderdale and reentered classes there for the remainder of the eleventh grade. She wasted no time calling her friends to announce her return.

"My first Sunday morning back at church, I knelt at the altar rail. A sunbeam flitted through a small window to my left, as if God himself was sending me a message." Lucy recalls feeling a peace that she didn't even know she needed.

Looking back on those tender teen years, Lucy is grateful for the freedom from stuttering.

"My mother and daddy finally realized that Ft. Lauderdale was the place where we would spend the rest of my school days until I graduated."

Looking back on those tender teen years, Lucy is grateful for the freedom from stuttering. "It brings much joy to my life. I cannot identify which event was my actual turning point though. Was it the psychiatrist's advice? Caring parents who wanted to help me? High school friends who welcomed me? A gentle English teacher?"

She doesn't need an official explanation, because she knows that a loving God directed the whole event. "I see it plainly written in Scripture whenever I read Jeremiah 29:11: 'For I know the plans I have for you,' declares the Lord, 'plans to prosper you and not to harm you, plans to give you hope and a future.'"

The Transformation

God has given us two hands,
one to receive with and the other to give with.

—BILLY GRAHAM

"It is a proven fact that every person needs fatherly love and affection during his childhood years. I was not so fortunate," says Roy.

Roy has never figured out why he never seemed to live up to his dad's expectations. "Perhaps it was because I was tenderhearted and shrank away from fighting my own battles. How could a father be proud of that?"

His dad was never one for handing out compliments. Roy doesn't remember any physical or verbal affection. Instead, he recalls negative labels and verbal abuse. "He placed me in situations in which I could not succeed. For instance, we planted a five-acre field of potatoes, and it was my assigned job to care for them. Every time I approached that plot of ground, the task appeared overwhelming."

His father didn't provide tools, so all Roy had was his own two hands. The impossible task led to repeated confrontations centering around that potato field. "Most of my emotional life was consumed with hatred toward my dad," Roy admits. In spite of the tension between them, Roy knew deep down that they loved each other, but the lack of this love's expression formed a strained father-son relationship.

> ALTHOUGH HE LEARNED TO GET ALONG RELATIVELY WELL WITH HIS FATHER, A DEEP-ROOTED HATRED PERSISTED.

After Roy became an adult, he moved away from home. When he started a family of his own, he insisted that his parents get along if they were going to visit. "My home was not going to be a verbal battleground," he says. Although he learned to get along relatively well with his father, a deep-rooted hatred persisted. He couldn't seem to shake it.

"My parents visited our home only a few times, but their last visit turned their lives around." During this visit, they attended church with Roy and his family. It was a loving congregation, and as Roy recalls, "It was amusing to see that these two warriors were attracted to the people there. They seemed to long for the love that neither one of them had ever experienced before."

When his mother developed Lou Gehrig's disease, people from the church blessed her in countless ways. During that difficult period in her life, Roy was surprised to learn that she had accepted the Lord as her Savior while in junior high school. "As far as I recall, she had never shared that with anyone," says Roy. Confident that she had passed into Heaven, Roy made a point of planning his mother's funeral as a victory celebration.

The greatest change in Roy's life, however, involved his relationship with his dad. "There came a time when I wanted so much to express every bit of hatred for him that had built up over the years. As we sat alone in his motor home, I started to organize my words."

Before he had a chance to uncap his frustration, a still, small voice interrupted his thoughts: *Put your arms around him and say that you love him.* He obeyed, and his destructive emotions left immediately. "God released me from the hatred that had sapped my strength for most of my life."

> IT WAS THE LOVE OF GOD THAT TURNED AN ORNERY MAN INTO A GENTLEMAN.

He and his dad talked well into the night. It was the first time the two of them had ever relaxed and hung out with each other. He remembers wondering, *Is this really happening?* As time went on, it was obvious that God was at work creating a new life—a new father-son relationship.

"It was the love of God that turned an ornery man into a gentleman," says Roy. "Nothing else would ever have made such an impossible change. Dad lived without my mother for the last year of his life. Oddly enough, I saw it as the best period of his life."

Roy and his dad spent long stretches of time together. They met for lunch as often as possible, and as strange as it seemed after their rocky history, he thoroughly enjoyed his dad's company. One event stands out above all others—evidence of God's grace at work in a heart. "The most precious memory I have of Dad is during the times of worship we shared together. My heart nearly stopped one day as the ugliest man I ever knew raised his hands in humble submission to the Lord." The sight of his dad worshiping in spirit and in truth is unforgettable.

Roy's greatest honor was to speak at his father's funeral service. People expressed surprise at the great change that had taken place in their relationship. He summed up his eulogy by saying, "There lies my dad. He was a real gentleman whom I dearly loved."

Priceless Treasure

Do not have your concert first, and then tune your instrument afterwards. Begin the day with the Word of God and prayer, and get first of all into harmony with him.

—HUDSON TAYLOR

Parenting isn't for the fainthearted. It's hard work and rarely ever resembles the images presented in those cozy commercials that depict families laughing together around the breakfast table. In reality, parenthood is a revolving door of joy and frustration.

There was a time when her role as a mother and wife left Janey feeling despondent. "It just seemed that no matter how well-intentioned I tried to be, life didn't turn out the way I'd hoped. Parenting was becoming a real challenge."

Janey recalls one such challenge, during a long-awaited

family vacation in Italy. She and her family were living in France at the time, just three hours from the Italian border. Their special time together should have been perfect, but nothing seemed to turn out that way. At least that's how Janey viewed it.

There they were, surrounded by gorgeous mountains. A vibrant turquoise sea stretched out before them—the perfect setting for a "deliciously scorching afternoon on the Italian Riviera." *What could be better than that?* thought Janey.

> WHO WOULD HAVE THOUGHT THAT ONLY A FEW HOURS BEFORE, I WAS UMPIRING THEIR UMPTEENTH FIGHT OF THE MORNING?

Bright sunlight seeped into her imagination as she squinted at the serene scene before her. Her daughter, Rachèle, was swimming nearby; her long, golden, sun-streaked hair caressing the curves of the waves. It was a beautiful, almost surreal scene, and Janey felt as if she were witnessing a mermaid swimming delicately about.

But as peaceful as her daughter appeared in that picturesque paradise, it was only an illusion—totally opposite from the real picture. Rachèle's attitude earlier that morning had been far from serene. Onlookers at the beach would never have imagined the struggle Janey's daughter was experiencing as her ten-year-old mind explored preteen independence.

Rachèle's vivacious five-year-old brother, Francesco,

was bobbing in the waves next to her. His bronze skin seemed to blend in with brown rocks in the distance, like a painting of a lovely summer scene. He and his sister's giggles joined the splash of the surf to form a playful melody—a backdrop to Janey's ponderings.

Who would have thought that only a few hours before, I was umpiring their umpteenth fight of the morning? Janey thought, as she watched her kids frolicking in the surf. Her melancholy mood clashed with the lively scene before her, and she wondered, *Why does every morning have to begin on a battlefield? Why do Francesco and Rachèle always have to fight in spite of prayer and family time together in God's Word? And why do all those endless how-to books about Christian parenting leave me feeling so deflated?*

Janey glanced again at her children and whispered heavenward, "Help me raise these children!"

"This was the sincere cry of my worn-out mother's heart," she says. "I knew that God was the only one who could help us raise our children well."

Some pretty pebbles had washed up on the beach to interrupt her introspection. "Look, Mama! I found some very treasure!" Francesco called happily to his mother.

"Lovely, son!"

"That's so cute!" my husband whispered in my ear. "He thinks *very* treasure means *buried* treasure!"

Janey wasn't surprised by Francesco's response, because

she and the children had recently read the biblical parable about buried treasure. Ever since, her son had been referring to his sandy discoveries as "very treasure." She had decided not to correct him, because it was such a cute play on words.

"And here's some more, Mama!" yelled Francesco, holding up a fistful of pretty pebbles.

He laid the colored stones in three piles on her towel and pointed to each one. "This one is the treasure, those ones are the very treasure, and those are the very, very treasure!"

Janey clenched her jaw to keep from laughing. "We did not dare offend this serious little treasure hunter by chuckling. But with concealed amusement, my whole spirit felt lighter. Life suddenly seemed simpler, and the value of my own little treasures more apparent. At that moment, I felt as rich as royalty."

God used the innocent words of an enthusiastic child to touch Janey's weary soul. He reminded her that even when life is difficult, plenty of treasures await anyone who looks in the right place.

"That place is heavenward, toward the one who knows our hearts, feels our weariness, understands our pain, and shares the entire experience with us. He can take our doldrums and turn them into blessings. He can take our hard times and teach us to laugh again—if we'll only seek his help," says Janey.

And he can turn buried spiritual treasure into the very treasure we need, to help us maneuver through the challenges of each day.

The Ultimate Decorator

Lord, you have been our dwelling place
throughout all generations.

—PSALM 90:1

Arlene's a city girl. Her husband had taken early retirement, and they had been looking for a place where God could use them in full-time Christian service. When she heard about a possible move to a Christian retreat center in the snow belt, Arlene's immediate reaction was a horrified "No!" But after praying about it, they felt led to make a one-year commitment.

Cedar Bend Farm was located in a beautiful setting and consisted of ten rustic buildings: in the woods were three small shacks with dirt floors; a log cabin; a manor house; a chapel that seated about fifty; a barn full of animals; a shop for wood carving and weaving;

a gallery of beautiful handcrafted art; and an old pottery shed. The shed would serve as their home. The property also included stacks of canoes, rabbit cages, an area where the blacksmith worked, a cider mill, and a shed full of cross-country skiing equipment.

Life in the country proved to be busy. Herb societies toured the gardens regularly, and other visitors enjoyed watching craftsmen at work. Concerts and weddings took place in the chapel. Some visitors came simply to experience a time of solitude, while others came to ski, fish, or rent the manor house for family reunions or church retreats. Nearly 180 college students studied culture there each fall. They arrived in groups of thirty and stayed for two days. Every spring, elementary teachers scheduled day trips for their students as well.

Arlene knew that she would spend most of her time inside that converted pottery shed and would entertain company often. However, the decor left something to be desired. She loved when everything matched, but an outdated harvest gold stove and avocado green refrigerator shared a small kitchen with two differently colored cupboards. "White walls sported gaudy black electrical switch plates. Bright gold carpeting in the bedroom was mildewed and worn. Windows were bare, and the cottage's only source of heat was a wood stove with an old bent piece of tin standing behind it to protect the wall," says Arlene. And since they'd agreed to live there only one year, her husband didn't want her spending a lot of money decorating.

"Delight yourself in the Lord, and he will give you the desires of your heart" (Psalm 37:4) took on new meaning that September. Arlene truly was delighting in serving the Lord and was willing to live under rough conditions, but God knew how much she appreciated beautiful surroundings. So behind the scenes, he went to work on the details.

> "DELIGHT YOURSELF IN THE LORD, AND HE WILL GIVE YOU THE DESIRES OF YOUR HEART" (PSALM 37:4) TOOK ON NEW MEANING THAT SEPTEMBER.

The owner said he would pay for any fixing up they wanted to do, so they bought paint and replaced the bedroom carpet. Arlene painted the refrigerator and installed new electrical socket covers in a soft shade of ivory to match her newly painted walls. Her husband built roomy shelves for their kitchen and covered the wall behind the wood stove with an attractive brick facing. The pottery shed was beginning to look like home.

One day, Arlene walked into a closeout store and spotted floral curtains that matched her couch and love seat perfectly—same flowers, same colors—for only $4.95 a pair! Walking out of the store, she noticed several lumpy pillows on clearance for 99 cents each—another perfect match. She took them apart, and her creative daughter-in-law made seat covers for their kitchen chairs. The pillows had been stuffed with matching fabric scraps, which she used to create a beautiful patchwork runner and a matching wreath. Another daughter-in-law bought a gift of coordinating place mats she "happened" to see on a trip to another state.

Arlene combined older plain-colored curtains, valances, and tiebacks with her new floral curtains for a striking effect. Each time new people entered their home that year, they commented on its beautiful decor. "That might seem small in comparison with world problems," says Arlene, "but I know my heavenly Father enjoyed surprising his child with all those fun details." Each visitor's compliment opened an opportunity for Arlene to share how God had provided.

God had confirmed to the city girl that he wanted her in that exact place. He not only met their practical house-related needs that year, he also generously blessed her

> EACH VISITOR'S COMPLIMENT OPENED AN OPPORTUNITY FOR ARLENE TO SHARE HOW GOD HAD PROVIDED.

with good friends, ministry opportunities, and plenty of time to develop new interests. Arlene led a community Bible study in their home, attended her first writing conference, and wrote her first book.

Then like a seasonal shift, her health began to deteriorate. Steeped in pain and nearly housebound, Arlene would glance around her cozy home and feel God's comforting presence.

"My heavenly Father and I have great times together," she says. "When I look at the beautiful things he made here on earth, I can hardly wait to see how he has decorated Heaven."

Faith Encounters Faithfulness

The most eloquent prayer is the prayer through hands that heal and bless. The highest form of worship is the worship of unselfish Christian service. The greatest form of praise is the sound of consecrated feet seeking out the lost and helpless.

—BILLY GRAHAM

Christian's faith laid a firm foundation for his life, yet it wasn't until a period of severe testing that he truly believed nothing could ever take it away. He'd been serving as a missionary in Mexico. There he had met Norma, who would later become his wife. Shortly after their marriage, Christian and Norma moved to a different location in order to begin a new church.

"We established a Bible study group, which had been meeting for several months. Suddenly everything began to unravel," says Christian. Some of the people moved away, and others simply stopped attending. In spite of their efforts, numbers continued to fall.

During that same time frame, Norma became pregnant with their first child, a baby boy. "Our doctor ordered her to be on complete bed rest during the pregnancy. Our financial support from the U.S. also evaporated quite suddenly." It seemed as though everything was caving in on them.

> SUDDENLY EVERYTHING BEGAN TO UNRAVEL.

Christian felt it was time to look for other ways in which to serve God. He prayed hard for direction and kept his eyes open for work that would allow him to also remain in the ministry. However, every door seemed to slam shut.

"I made the painful decision to step down from the ministry in order to take care of my family," he says. The resulting backlash surprised him. "Friends from back home criticized me. The emotional and spiritual agony I felt was indescribable."

His most dismal day came when he had to choose between spending the remainder of their household money on food or medication. Norma had gone into premature labor and needed medicine to prevent miscarriage. "I chose to protect the baby and bought medicine instead of food. One day Norma asked me to buy food, and I walked away in tears. How could I tell my bedridden wife that I had spent every cent we had?"

As he sought answers from God, Christian heard a knock at the door. It was his mother-in-law coming for a visit. He tearfully opened the door and welcomed her inside. "For a few moments, I didn't realize that she had set several bags of groceries on the table. She said she was going to the corner store to buy tortillas. My in-laws are among the poorest of the poor, so this was a huge sacrifice."

At their exact moment of need, God provided. "Every time we ran out of food, God

AT THEIR EXACT MOMENT OF NEED, GOD PROVIDED.

sent someone to us with food, or sent us money to buy a small amount of food ourselves. We learned to depend on him and totally trust that he would provide our daily needs."

God's grace continued to flow. First, a friend gave Christian a pickup truck that had been totaled in a crash. "He had restored it to good working condition so I could have transportation to seek work across the border in the United States." The only available work he found was as a public school teacher. "I started as a substitute but was quickly offered a full-time contract for the following school year," says Christian.

The most amazing part of God's provision is that the school district didn't have an opening when he first applied. According to Christian, they bypassed the normal hiring procedures and created a job for him. "While some teachers insinuated that I had played politics to get a job that didn't exist, I knew the truth. The only 'politics' involved were God's politics."

The job included benefits that would help pay for his son's birth. "The school district kept me working daily at substitute pay until God stepped in again," recalls Christian. "Two days after my son was born, more than three-quarters of the way through the school year, the school district decided to have me begin working full-time with full benefits immediately; they canceled the usual five-month waiting period."

Christian looks back on those distressing days as a picture of God's faithfulness. "There is no doubt in my mind that God cares about his children. He provides day by day. I've lived it! Yes, I was heartbroken by circumstances, but sometimes God allows us to suffer heartbreak for our own spiritual benefit."

In turn, God uses each of us as a tool for ministry to others who may be experiencing equally tough times. Because he experienced a difficult season of life, Christian believes that the Lord will continue to use him to bless others in similar circumstances.

"It was never about my faith, but about God's faithfulness and love."

FORTY-TWO

Waiting in the Wilderness

Look to the Lord and his strength; seek his face always.

—1 CHRONICLES 16:11

"You do want children, don't you?" Candy's eyes blurred with tears. Whenever she heard those words, she felt wounded all over again. How could she answer calmly, when her heart wanted to scream?

This wasn't the first time she'd been asked such a question. She had encountered the probing before—much too frequently, in fact. To make matters even more difficult, lately it seemed that Candy ran into pregnant women everywhere she went. "My life was full of pregnant ladies. I was not one of them. Pregnancy, which for many seemed to happen by accident (or as was often joked about among our circle of friends, from drinking the tea of a local drive-in restaurant), had somehow eluded me."

Conceiving a child had become a source of daily concern for Candy. After eight months of dutifully taking her temperature in the predawn hours each morning and charting the results, she and her husband decided to take the next step. They sought the help of a gynecologist and launched into a regimen of infertility testing. It would prove to be a long journey.

"For months I endured testing, biopsies, and pelvic exams. Finally, laparoscopic surgery revealed endometriosis, a condition that causes infertility," says Candy. The treatment itself is not stressful. "We learned that our best option would require nine months of drug therapy during which I must not become pregnant because of the risk of massive birth defects."

> HOW COULD SHE ANSWER CALMLY, WHEN HER HEART WANTED TO SCREAM?

"This was one of the most difficult times in our journey. I approached the drug treatment and its related side effects with impatience, but held on to the hope that within a few months after finishing the therapy, I would be able to conceive."

It didn't happen.

The next step would be another round of fertility drugs plus artificial insemination. Candy felt that her life had become an emotional roller coaster. "Spiritually, I had shut down. I tried to maintain a regular Bible study and prayer life, but one night as I lay in bed, I remember shouting to God, 'My prayers are reaching no higher than the ceiling! They're bouncing back and hitting me in the face. Where are you, God?'"

She recalls a moment the next day when despair covered her like a dark cloud. She reached for her Bible and read the words of Psalm 37:4 with new eyes: "Delight yourself in the Lord and he will give you the desires of your heart."

A FEW DAYS BEFORE VALENTINE'S DAY, CANDY AND HER HUSBAND PACED AROUND THEIR BEDROOM, AWAITING THE RESULTS OF A PREGNANCY TEST.

Though her heart's greatest desire was to have a baby, Candy knew she had to face the raw truth: "I was not delighted in the Lord or anyone else. I definitely had some issues that needed work."

Several Sundays later, their pastor's message happened to center on the story of Hannah, a woman who longed for a child. The words of 1 Samuel 1 spoke directly to Candy's heart, as if they'd been written especially for her. "Peninnah had children, but Hannah had none" (v. 2). Hannah wept and prayed, prayed and wept until God finally blessed her with a baby boy.

A flicker of hope ignited in Candy. Could it be that God was working to teach her what it means to wait patiently?

A few days before Valentine's Day, Candy and her husband paced around their bedroom, awaiting the results of a pregnancy test. "We tiptoed to the bathroom door after the required time had elapsed and peeked around the corner," she says. "Our whoops of joy echoed throughout the house when we saw the blue stick indicating a positive test result. Our deepest prayers had been answered!"

Their long-awaited baby arrived early on an autumn morning. Today she is a beautiful teenager with curly brown hair, smiling eyes, and a zest for life.

Nearly three and a half years after their daughter's birth, following another round of fertility drugs and artificial insemination, God added a son to the family. Candy knows without a doubt that each of her children is the fulfillment of her heart's desire—a gift from God.

Maturity develops through disappointment and heartache, and Candy praises God for his faithfulness during that growth process. "My time of wandering in the wilderness of infertility taught me the importance of trusting God and waiting patiently before him."

With the passing of years, she has learned to appreciate the benefits of that long wait. "We grew closer as a couple, and we developed compassionate, tender, and understanding hearts for those who bear the pain—and often the shame—of infertility. Because of our bittersweet experience, we are able to offer hope and encouragement to them."

FORTY-THREE

Refreshed by Peace

Worry does not empty tomorrow of its sorrow;
it empties today of its strength.

—CORRIE TEN BOOM

L ife as we know it can shift without warning, over-whelming us with its impact. Several years ago, in the wee hours of a May morning, Donna cried out to God and experienced a life-changing response.

On Sunday, her pastor husband, Don, had preached with his characteristic enthusiasm. "Something akin to an aerobic workout," says Donna. "The day before, he'd jogged, planted roses, and prepared his messages." Tired from preaching two sermons, Don usually retired early, but not on this particular night. She found him still awake at 1:00 AM, sitting in the dark. After persistent questioning, he admitted that he felt pain in his back and jaw.

Donna reached for the phone to dial 911, and he protested. "I'll be fine."

Their teenage daughter, Leah, stepped into the room to see what was going on, and wasted no time confronting her father. "Dad! Your own dad died from a heart attack at the age of forty-nine. Do you want to take that chance?"

They convinced him to let Donna drive him to the emergency room. All the way to the hospital, her mind raced ahead. *What if he goes into full-blown cardiac arrest and collapses? Oh, Lord, please help me get him to the hospital!*

The details of that night are forever carved in Donna's memory. The next few hours were filled with tests, followed by an ambulance to a nearby city, where a specialist was waiting to perform bypass surgery. "I filled out enough forms to wallpaper my house; made arrangements for our two children; and called family, friends, and work. I found out that, although I couldn't stay in the room with Don, I could stay in the hospital, so I made a reservation for a room."

Tired from preaching two sermons, Don usually retired early, but not on this particular night.

She stayed several doors away from the main hallway, in an abandoned wing of the hospital. It was nearly two o'clock in the morning on Tuesday. She had not slept since Saturday night.

Exhausted and alone, Donna fell into bed but couldn't

sleep. "After all the hustle and bustle and the myriad of machines beeping in the ICU downstairs, my silent room seemed oppressive," she relates. "The enormity of the situation hit me, and I began to sob. What if Don didn't survive? What would I do without him?"

If Don didn't pull through, their son, Aaron, would always relate his birthday to the day his father had heart surgery. And Leah's high school graduation was less than three weeks away. "In a few short years, we faced the possibility of an empty nest. We had laughed and talked about the freedom that would afford us. Now I might lose Don too."

> BEFORE SHE HAD FINISHED HER PRAYER, SHE SENSED GOD'S WARM, COMFORTING PRESENCE.

Donna had never felt so alone. "Oh, God, help me!" she cried. Before she had finished her prayer, she sensed God's warm, comforting presence. "It felt as if warm oil had dripped from above, covering me from head to toe. The Holy Spirit seemed to expand and fill that lonely room. I felt the presence of the Lord as I'd never experienced him before."

Donna recalled a passage from the Bible in which the apostle Paul had told the Philippians, "Do not be anxious about anything, but in everything, by prayer and petition, with thanksgiving, present your requests to God. And the peace of God, which transcends all understanding, will guard your hearts and your minds in Christ Jesus" (Philippians 4:6, 7).

God stepped into her uncertainty and fear to cover her with his peace. "I knew that even if Don were to step into Heaven, God would be with me. I managed to sleep for about four hours. During the long day ahead, I leaned on family and friends and consoled my children. When fear threatened to overcome me, I allowed the Holy Spirit to refresh my spirit as I prayed."

The Lord sent people to encourage the family as well. "One family friend showed up with gourmet pizzas," says Donna. "Another close friend even thought to bring a cupcake to the waiting room for Aaron's birthday, and we sang a hushed version of 'Happy Birthday' to him."

Later that afternoon, the surgeon arrived with good news. He assured them that although Don had needed five bypasses, everything had gone well. He would be back to normal in no time.

"And he was," Donna confirms. "He made it to Leah's graduation a few weeks later, and he's back to his aerobic preaching!"

In her hour of need, God refreshed her with a peace that overshadowed her fear. Donna still clings to his faithfulness. "I know I'm never alone. I praise the Lord for his omnipresence and for the peace and comfort he brings when we call on his name."

Grace in the Backyard

Prayer is as natural an
expression of faith as breathing is of life.

—JONATHAN EDWARDS

Diane will always remember the day Paul and Linda moved into the neighborhood, with a cat and three dogs. She instantly recognized something special about the "Heinz 57" named Annie.

"Her intelligent eyes sized up anyone who stepped close to the fence," says Diane. "She'd sniff at the wind for danger signs, while her black tail signaled an alert. If you didn't belong, she would let everyone know."

But Annie was old now, and each day found her growing sicker. She ambled around the yard, guarding each feeble step. When translated into human years, Annie's fifteen years pointed to a long life. Still, who was ready to give up such a special friend?

One day in June, Diane wandered over to Linda's house for a visit. As usual, Annie rose slowly, barked, and then escorted her through the gate.

Linda welcomed Diane into the kitchen and handed her a steaming cup of coffee.

"Where did you come up with the name Annie?" Diane wondered aloud.

Linda laughed. "Oh, we celebrated our first wedding anniversary by adopting a dog from the animal shelter. We called her Annie—short for anniversary."

They talked about how Annie had naturally protected her family and friends right from the beginning. "She raised a neighborhood of children, stalked numerous snakes, and kept trespassers away," says Diane.

Annie had weathered many changes as children were added to their household. When an assortment of canine and feline friends later joined her, she simply expanded her protective borders to accommodate them.

WHEN TRANSLATED INTO HUMAN YEARS, ANNIE'S FIFTEEN YEARS POINTED TO A LONG LIFE.

After they had chatted awhile, it was time for Diane to go. She stepped outside and saw Annie struggle to get up. "She hadn't heard me close the front door, but wagged her tail and gazed at me through hazy eyes." Diane recognized the fact that Annie probably wouldn't be around much longer.

Paul and Linda's children noticed the change in their beloved pet too.

EVEN THOUGH THEY FELT NO DOG COULD MEASURE UP TO ANNIE, THE FAMILY BEGAN PRAYING FOR A NEW DOG THAT WOULD MIX WELL WITH THEIR OTHER ANIMALS.

"Papa, is it wrong to pray for us to get another dog while Annie is still alive?" one of them asked. They realized the family needed a watch-dog, but the children didn't want to seem disloyal.

"No," Paul assured them. "God knows your heart."

Even though they felt no dog could measure up to Annie, the family began praying for a new dog that would mix well with their other animals. After prayers one night, their oldest child, Stephen, touched his father's sleeve.

"Papa, what kind of dog do you think God will send us?"

Paul ran his fingers through his hair and looked into each solemn face. "Well, I'm not sure, but I know in the past God provided the right pets at the right time."

Three other voices chimed in with questions and opinions, but Linda quieted them.

"It's time you scoot off to bed. God knows what he's doing; let's just wait and see, OK?"

GOD KNOWS
WHAT HE'S DOING;
LET'S JUST WAIT
AND SEE, OK?

By late July, Annie visited the vet twice. During her last visit, Linda and the children hovered around the table as Dr. Smith checked her over. He rubbed Annie between the ears. One by one the children reached out to pet her. They studied Dr. Smith's face for a clue—his expression relayed bad news.

"There's nothing I can do," he said, shaking his head. He stroked Annie's head again and turned to Linda. "Take her home. Do what you can. If she's in pain, call me."

A few days later, Annie barked until someone came outside.

"Annie seemed to be calling for companionship that Saturday, so we all went out to sit with her," explains Linda. "We settled in the grass near her. For more than forty-five minutes she went to each one, laying her head in a lap and then painfully moving on to someone else. She seemed to be loving us for the last time."

After a while, Annie headed for the bushes in the backyard and lay down. The family said good-night to her, but Paul and Linda knew it was really good-bye. Through the kitchen window, Linda's gaze settled on the bushes.

"When I checked on Annie the next morning, I knew she was dead. It broke my heart," says Linda. The family gathered to bury her. Each reminisced about a special memory they'd made with Annie.

The kids stayed home with their dad and played in the pool while Linda ran a few errands. She hadn't been gone ten minutes when Paul called her cell phone. He sounded excited.

"You won't believe what happened!"

Stephen had found a black puppy creeping out of the bushes close to where Annie had died.

Linda was in absolute awe of God's answer to her children's heartfelt prayers. "The puppy fits like a piece in a familiar puzzle. We named her Grace—God's gift at a difficult time."

Ties That Bind

Commit to the Lord whatever you do,
and your plans will succeed.

—PROVERBS 16:3

arbara's family is large and close-knit. When they all get together, they number well over fifty people. For as long as she can remember, her family has been her bedrock of support, a source of unconditional love. There's only one problem, though. "They all live in Maryland, and I live in South Carolina," says Barbara.

When people ask what brought her to South Carolina, so far from loved ones, she's at a loss for words. "I never made a conscious decision to live here. A company did not transfer me, and I had no family ties here. What I had was a best friend who, in a very dark season of my life, suggested that I stay with her until I could heal enough to make wise decisions. Seven years later, I am still here."

In the back of her mind, Barbara always planned to return home. In fact, she had attempted to move several

IN THE BACK OF HER MIND, BARBARA ALWAYS PLANNED TO RETURN HOME.

times in the past. "The first time, I had a job offer that would have doubled my salary. My brother took me house hunting, and I found the perfect town house. My family and old friends were jubilant."

But when Barbara awoke at her sister's home on the morning of her final interview for the new job, she knew in her heart that she was about to make a mistake. She packed her bags in a rush, told her family she was leaving, and headed back to South Carolina.

"As I drove south on I-95, I felt such a lightness of spirit. I put on some music as I entered Virginia where, as always, I did not have cell phone reception," says Barbara.

So when her cell phone somehow received a signal, Barbara was startled to hear it ring. It was her pastor, calling to say that God kept bringing her to mind. He had felt impressed to specifically ask the Lord to show her that it was not time for her to make a move yet. A few minutes later she tried to make a call, but once again, she couldn't receive a signal in that stretch of I-95.

As the years passed, her parents experienced the usual issues of aging. Health problems arose, and during one Christmas visit, Barbara was shocked by the physical changes that had taken place in them since her last visit. "Once again, I felt a pull toward home," she recalls. She tried to determine how many more times she would get to see them at the rate of two visits per year. It was a dismal math problem.

So a year after her first attempts to move home, she took a summer trip to decide once and for all. She prayed for a sign, visited friends and family, and tried to imagine herself living there. By the time an old friend accompanied her to church, Barbara felt thoroughly confused. All during the service, she prayed for clarity.

"Then God stepped in," says Barbara. "The pastor showed a video of Sara Groves singing 'Painting Pictures of Egypt,' and as I watched and listened, tears streamed down my cheeks." The song spoke of moving on instead of longing for the past. It gave her the assurance that God would use the things she had learned to build a bright future for her in South Carolina.

THE SONG SPOKE OF MOVING ON INSTEAD OF LONGING FOR THE PAST.

"My prayers for a sign had been answered; a burning bush could not have been clearer. There would be no return to family. Case closed. My new prayer became, 'Lord, show me what and why.'"

Much has happened in Barbara's life over the course of the past seven years. She accepted Jesus Christ as her Savior at Lamb's Chapel in Florence, South Carolina, and came to know the true meaning of a church family. "Total strangers loved me back to wellness, both spiritually and physically. They have stood with me during every trial and rejoiced with me over every victory," says Barbara. "They are my larger family here in Florence; they are in addition to, not instead of, my natural family."

GOD CALMED
HER RESTLESS SPIRIT.

Barbara has also learned that as God's children, we are like brothers and sisters in Christ. The true church is not a building—it's made up of believers.

God calmed her restless spirit. She now talks to her parents by phone several times each week and flies to visit them when she can. "All of the changes in my life, including the distance from loved ones, have brought us closer. My family ties have actually been strengthened."

Burden to Blessing

Dear children, let us not love with words or tongue
but with actions and in truth.

—1 JOHN 3:18

"**B**ut Mama, it's my baby!" wailed Katherine's seventeen-year-old daughter, Abby. Her face was red and puffy, streaked with tears.

"You don't have a husband, and once the baby is born, you probably won't have a home, either!" her mother snapped. "That child is NOT coming into this house!"

Abby's father was the new minister in town. In the eyes of their newly adopted community, biracial dating was strictly off limits. But Abby had fallen in love with a young black man. Aside from the issue of local prejudices, Abby's parents also questioned how she could have betrayed her upbringing. "What happened to your commitment to remain a virgin until marriage?" they asked.

Daily, tension mounted, dividing mother and daughter. Conversations turned into heated arguments.Whenever Abby mentioned keeping her baby, Katherine clearly reminded Abby that she had no intention of becoming a grandmother to "that" baby. "We can't possibly keep a biracial baby. We'll find an African-American family who wants to adopt. We just need to get past this so our lives can return to normal, that's all."

Stung by her mother's words, Abby raged, "Normal? Do you really think my life will ever be normal again?"

When her boyfriend heard the news of her pregnancy, he wanted nothing to do with her. Abby's heart sank. The humiliation was too much. With her mother by her side, she decided to enroll in a home for young pregnant women several hours away. There she would stay until her baby was born. Time away would give her the opportunity to both clear her head and complete her school year.

Katherine and her husband, Paul, found solace in the loving embrace of their church fellowship. No one condemned Abby or hinted that they had been bad parents. When summer arrived, they picked Abby up for a visit, with arrangements already in place for her to enter another maternity home for the remainder of her pregnancy. And what a visit it was!

That first morning back home in her own bed, Abby experienced early labor. A trip to the doctor confirmed that the situation was critical. "You'll need to stay in bed until this child is born," he told her.

Abby seemed happy at the prospect of staying at home, but Katherine reacted harshly. Her first thoughts were for herself and for what others might think. *"What? He wants her to stay put—in our home?"*

One night, Abby's contractions increased in length and intensity. Katherine stayed up all night timing them, and the next morning they headed to the hospital. However, progress was so slow, her doctor suggested that a C-section delivery might be necessary.

Katherine donned a sterile blue gown and stayed close by. When nurses coached Abby to push with all her might, she delivered a handsome baby boy. "His name is Timothy," whispered Abby.

A CASEWORKER HAD ALREADY ARRANGED FOR A FOSTER MOTHER TO ARRIVE AT THE HOSPITAL TO TAKE TIMOTHY.

Her joy was short-lived. A caseworker had already arranged for a foster mother to arrive at the hospital to take Timothy the next morning. Abby was allowed one bottle-feeding before handing him over.

Early the next morning, Katherine stood off to one side in the hospital lobby as her grandson was whisked away.

Abby returned home that afternoon, sank into a recliner, and sighed, "Things will never be the same again." In the days ahead, her prediction seemed to be accurate. Katherine witnessed her daughter's intense battle with grief. *Her body will heal,* thought Katherine, *but how long will it take her heart to mend?*

As Timothy's birth mother, Abby was given a fifteen-day grace period to decide whether to officially give up her parental rights. But surprisingly, it was Katherine whose heart was most torn. While reading her Bible one morning, she came across an unusual question in 1 Corinthians 1:20: "Where is the wise man? Where is the scholar? Where is the philosopher of this age? Has not God made foolish the wisdom of the world?"

God's Word seemed to wash over her layers of fear, and she tearfully confessed her prejudice and hypocrisy. She and Paul agreed that their grandson didn't need a new home; he already had one—there with them.

At the supper table, Paul reached for his daughter's hand. "Timothy is welcome here in our home, Abby. Would you like to make a phone call?"

> GOD'S AMAZING GRACE HAD TRANSFORMED A HEAVY BURDEN INTO ONE OF LIFE'S MOST BEAUTIFUL BLESSINGS.

Months of confusion melted away as the three of them hugged, cried, and rejoiced together.

Years later, Katherine can still picture the moment when a caring foster mother placed baby Timothy back into Abby's waiting arms. The same little outfit he had worn at their tearful good-bye would be forever captured in their homecoming photos. God's amazing grace had transformed a heavy burden into one of life's most beautiful blessings.

FORTY-SEVEN

Field of Green

All I have seen teaches me
to trust the Creator for all I have not seen.
—RALPH WALDO EMERSON

Twila would soon be turning thirty. *I wonder what God has in store for me,* she thought wistfully. After all, David had become king, Joseph had become Pharaoh's right-hand man, and Jesus had begun his ministry by the age of thirty.

Three years earlier, Twila had lost her dad to a brain tumor and her husband to another woman. "Though God had healed me immensely since that time, it was obvious that he was still gently peeling away layers of hurt that I had padded around myself as a protective measure. Only recently my prayers had changed from 'Lord, please keep me from pain and deception' to 'Lord, please expose my pain and deception and heal it.'"

God answered Twila in clear, loving terms that she could readily grasp: *Hold on. Just wait. I will fix you.*

"At the beginning of April, I visited my mom in northeast Missouri, where the swelling tulips and redbuds were nearing the day when they would burst into full bloom. In the past, I had always enjoyed the fact that the beautiful colors reached their peak on my birthday," says Twila.

Within the past year, she'd moved to Florida and become what some would call a city girl, but Twila always loved returning to this slower-paced, small-town, farming community. She often took leisurely walks around town, taking in the familiar countryside of proud old homes, lush trees, and fields where her ancestors—and her roots—were buried.

THREE YEARS EARLIER, TWILA HAD LOST HER DAD TO A BRAIN TUMOR AND HER HUSBAND TO ANOTHER WOMAN.

Though she'd returned home many times in the past few years, this particular April visit stirred a collection of painful memories. "I slept in the same room where only a few years ago, I'd wrestled with the loss of the two most important men in my life," recalls Twila. "One night, I lay there unable to sleep, knowing that only a few feet from my bed, a drawer of old photos remained untouched since that painful period in my life. Confused at why God was allowing all this junk to surface, and disappointed that I had no resolution, I sought answers from him. He met me with silence."

The next morning, she left with barely a word to her mother, and set off on a trek into the countryside with her head and heart in turmoil. It was chilly, and she walked quickly, hardly noticing her surroundings. While Twila believed in God and knew that he answers prayer, she finally admitted that she thought he had turned his back on her. Why else would one person have had to endure so much pain and loss?

> WHILE TWILA BELIEVED IN GOD AND KNEW THAT HE ANSWERS PRAYER, SHE FINALLY ADMITTED THAT SHE THOUGHT HE HAD TURNED HIS BACK ON HER.

"In anguish, I silently begged God to answer me right there and then. I asked him to give me a word, a mental picture, a memory, a song—something tangible to prove that he heard me and loved me enough to respond. I stood still in the middle of that gravel road, eyes shut, straining every nerve for some sort of divine affirmation," says Twila.

A picture formed in her mind—a burnt, blackened field that she had walked past only a couple of minutes before. "In my mind's eye, I viewed the field as if I were in an airplane, swooping low over the field toward the tree row in the distance."

Two days later, Twila set out on another walk. The sunny morning was abloom with redbuds, the air alive with birdsong. As she walked, Twila recalled God's faithfulness in answering other prayers. She remembered his earlier message: *Hold on. Just wait. I will fix you.* Twila admitted that she had formed a bad habit of limiting God—of putting him in a box, where she demanded immediate answers on her terms.

"I confessed all of this to God, surrendering to whatever he wanted to do in my life." She finished her prayer and glanced up for the first time since she'd left the house.

A FLOOD OF EMOTION WASHED OVER HER AS GOD FILLED HER HEART WITH THANKSGIVING.

Her eyes scanned brilliant green stretching out for acres. "At that moment, I suddenly realized that I was looking out over the same field that had been blackened just two days before! The rains had brought about a lush carpet of new growth, bright and glistening in the morning light."

A flood of emotion washed over her as God filled her heart with thanksgiving. She sensed him saying, *I did hear when you cried out to me. I answered you at that very moment. I am there beside you, even when you cannot sense my presence, busy working below ground level to heal and grow you. I am transforming your scorched, barren life into something that will unexpectedly burst forth into full bloom. Hold on. Just wait. I will fix you.*

Moments with My Maker

God doesn't look at how much we do,
but with how much love we do it.

—MOTHER TERESA

"I could tell it was going to be one of those days. I was weepy, hormonal, cranky, and generally out of sorts," says Dena. "I'd been cooped up in the house with two kids, I had a work deadline breathing down my neck, and I could feel a sinus infection coming on."

Earlier that morning, she had been cuddling on the bed with seven-year-old Jordan and two-year-old Jackson, when Jordan piped up with, "Jackson is so cute I could die!"

Dena says everything went downhill after that. Later that day, the boys were playing with markers—washable, of course. "At one point, I glanced over to see that Jordan had scribbled 'Kick me' on Jackson's lower back, just above his diaper. I had to laugh, but I also had to work at getting the so-called washable marker off with an unscheduled bath."

Jackson spent the rest of his tattooed day screaming at the top of his lungs. He flung his diaper off at every opportunity and would run away from Dena, laughing hysterically as only a two-year-old can do. "Poo-poo head!" he'd giggle.

> I WAS WEEPY, HORMONAL, CRANKY, AND GENERALLY OUT OF SORTS.

Over the course of a single day, Dena found herself handing out such remarkable advice as:

> "Your diaper is not a storage facility for raisins."
> "Don't drink the bathwater."
> "Don't lick the carpet."
> "Your nose is not the place for popcorn."
> "Yes, the people who live on Pluto probably do have lunch plans."

"By two o'clock, I was done in," says Dena. "And I still had a deadline to meet."

When Jackson's nap time arrived, she tried to work, but insecurity went to work instead. She thought of a negative review she'd received, and her mind went into an immediate tailspin. The harder she tried to work, the louder the voice of doubt became. "I realized that this was one of those times when I needed to just be still. I turned off the computer and poured myself a cup of hot chai tea."

FUNNY, SHE THOUGHT, MY LIFE HASN'T CHANGED ALL THAT MUCH IN THE PAST FEW MONTHS.

She sat in her favorite chair and opened her journal. *Funny*, she thought, *my life hasn't changed all that much in the past few months.* One entry read:

> Jordan brought me two dead crickets, a fake silver fingernail, and (oh yes!) some crumpled rose petals from the bush in the backyard last week. He also recently told his dad, "When I was two and three, I peed in the bath." When his dad looked at him incredulously and asked why in the world he would do that, Jordan said, "Well, it was too warm to get out when I had to go." Yikes! And when we were in the drive-through at McDonald's, I heard him say to his one-year-old brother, "You're supposed to toot when I pull your finger."

Dena couldn't help but laugh. "I'm in for a long haul, I'm afraid," she sighs. "It reminds me of something a friend shared with me recently. Her teenage son had advised her to check up on his younger brother, Matt, after he showered. When his mom asked why, he confessed, 'All through middle school, I never once used soap.'"

Dena thought of her own two boys who often drove her crazy. She'd often asked herself, *Hey, who needs sitcoms or the funny papers? I have two sons!*

Dena curled up in the chair and reached for her Bible. Whenever she felt insecure or frustrated, she'd often turn to the book of Isaiah. She loved 26:3, which reads, "You will keep in perfect peace him whose mind is steadfast, because he trusts in you." Those words always had a way of lifting her spirits and easing the frustration of the day.

> I NEED THOSE MOMENTS WITH MY MAKER TO REMIND ME THAT MY BOYS ARE BLESSINGS.

"Once again, I was comforted and encouraged by the Word and by being in God's presence," remarks Dena. "I didn't hear any audible voices or bells ringing, but like I told my husband later, 'The crazies went away.' I was able to regain my sense of sanity and realize that it's OK to feel nuts once in a while. God loves me anyway."

Dena knows that time with God "in the midst of mommy-hood" helps her to slow down and see the work God's doing in her life. "Spending time with him reminds me that with his strength, wisdom, and constant help, I'm doing the best I can in the role he has given me. I need those moments with my maker to remind me that my boys are blessings."

After taking time out to be with God, she is able to view her day from his perspective. Dena claims he also helps her discover great places to hide those "washable" markers!

The God of Miracles

*In prayer it is better to have a heart without words
than words without a heart.*

—JOHN BUNYAN

Pete remembers Bill as a likable guy with a big smile and an outstretched hand. "He never knew a stranger because he had such a kind heart and a sweet spirit. He lived the life of a godly man. But even godly men get cancer, and that is exactly what happened to Bill."

Bill held an important company position for an electrical contractor. He was the one who projected how high they should bid for the jobs they wanted. If he estimated too low, the company took a real hit. If he bid too high, they didn't get the job. The future of the company often rested squarely on Bill's capable shoulders.

"But in the midst of this busy schedule, Bill discovered

that he had cancer of the throat," says Pete. "The doctor told him it was serious and that he needed to get to Iowa City immediately for treatment."

Bill felt torn between his urgent health problem and his responsibilities at work.

"Bill was a member of the church where I ministered," says Pete. "Iowa City was about 110 miles away from his home. The mileage became a bit of a problem for his wife, Cyril, so whenever I traveled to see Bill, she would ride along with me."

> HE TOLD BILL,
> "WE NEED TO PRAY.
> I DON'T HAVE ANY ANSWERS,
> BUT GOD DOES."

Pete describes a memorable Monday morning when he and Cyril walked into Bill's hospital room. "We knew immediately that something was wrong. Instead of a smile on Bill's face, we saw deep despair. The cancer treatment had been hard on him, and in addition, he had become blind in one eye."

Bill didn't see how he was going to be able to drive ever again. Tired and frustrated, he spoke through tears. "I just wish the Lord would take me home."

Pete felt like his friend was sinking into a deep depression. He told Bill, "We need to pray. I don't have any answers, but God does."

As they prayed together, God's presence became very real to them. "When I finished praying I felt like I was standing on holy ground," Pete remembers.

Bill had a roommate, and Cyril introduced Pete to him. "This is my husband's minister," she said. When the man invited Pete to pray with him, Pete was more than happy to do so.

"No sooner had I begun than Cyril came around the curtain weeping," recalls Pete. "She said, 'Come quick! You have to see Bill.'"

Pete rushed back around the curtain and found Bill sitting up in bed reading his Sunday school papers. He was crying out, "I can see! Look! I can see out of my blind eye!"

The man in the bed next to Bill had also received cancer treatment, and the doctors had done all they could for him. "They were sending him home that very day, and they'd given him two weeks to live."

When the gentleman heard about Bill's returning eyesight, he grabbed Pete's hand and wanted him to finish praying with him right then. Shortly after their prayer, the ambulance crew arrived to transport him home. At nearly the same moment, a doctor stopped by to check on his patient and also to speak with Bill.

After studying Bill's chart, he wore a somber expression and declared, "Bill, I am sorry there is nothing we can do about your eye. It was probably a blood clot, but I feel the damage has already been done. I am so sorry."

Bill stopped him almost in mid-sentence. "God took care of it. He healed it!" The doctor backed out of the room shaking his head. He later returned with a nurse and confirmed what Bill had said: he could see!

About a month later, Pete was walking up a hospital corridor when someone laid a hand on his shoulder from behind. "I turned around and was amazed. It was the man I had prayed for in Bill's room. He was up walking, and he told me that the doctors had said his cancer was now in remission. They couldn't explain how or why."

> ABOUT A MONTH LATER, PETE WAS WALKING UP A HOSPITAL CORRIDOR WHEN SOMEONE LAID A HAND ON HIS SHOULDER FROM BEHIND.

The hospital chaplain asked Pete to come and speak to the nursing students. He wanted them to know that God always has the final word, no matter how bleak the prognosis. He wanted them to know that miracles do still happen.

Pete has prayed with people over the course of many years. He has seen countless answers to prayer, but has never had an experience quite like that day in Bill's room. "Bill was changed, the man in the bed next to him was changed, and so was I," says Pete. "Truly our God is a God of miracles!"

Truth in the Trenches

He gives strength to the weary
and increases the power of the weak.

—ISAIAH 40:29

Entering a writing contest wasn't supposed to lead to the emergency room, but that's where Cathy eventually ended up. She'd secretly entered a Christian competition that promised to send its winner on a trip to New York, with a free coaching session from professional writers. She hadn't traveled much since marrying Wayne; two preschoolers and two hundred ewes had quickly become her life. Winning a writing contest sounded like a good excuse for a vacation.

So she worked on her story in the evenings, carefully guarding her secret so no one would suspect. She mailed off her entry, then felt summer slow its pace as she anxiously awaited the day the winners would be announced. When that day arrived, Cathy hurried to her mailbox to retrieve the letter that would congratulate the contest winners.

What—no letter? How could that be? Hadn't the detailed entry stated that winners would be informed today? She plopped down on the couch, feeling dejected and confused. "God, I'm sorry," she prayed. "I guess I was writing more for myself than for you. I know I keep trying to control things."

> SHE PLOPPED DOWN ON THE COUCH, FEELING DEJECTED AND CONFUSED.

Letting go of her own will and accepting God's didn't happen overnight. Life was about to dole out a series of events that would showcase God's grace. First, their roof began to leak. "Friends volunteered to help," says Cathy, "and my husband, Wayne, went outside to gather supplies. I was helping dress Travis, our two-year-old, when Wayne hurried back inside."

"Could you look at my eye?" he asked. "I think I got something in it."

"I noticed a star-shaped wound not far from his iris," explains Cathy. "We rushed to the hospital, where a doctor carefully scooped out metal fragments."

Then he delivered the news that Wayne would need surgery ASAP. "I don't know whether we'll be able to save his eye where the nail penetrated tissue."

Cathy's knees shook as she walked to the public phone to call a close friend. She remembers choking back tears as she delivered her news. "Afterwards, I pressed my face against the wall and admitted my helplessness before God. 'Lord, thy will be done, even if it means Wayne may lose his eye,' I prayed."

Wayne was taken into surgery. Ninety minutes passed without any word. Two hours. Still no updates. "By then it was past 11:00 PM," remembers Cathy. Why was the surgery taking so long? How long would her commitment to "thy will be done" last?

> CATHY'S RESOLVE TO "THY WILL BE DONE" WAS TOUGHER THAN SHE'D ANTICIPATED, AND THE WEEK AHEAD WOULD PRESENT YET ANOTHER CHALLENGE.

Three hours later, Wayne's surgeon stepped into the waiting room. "The nail head entered your husband's eye at an odd angle. It'll take a week before we'll know whether we've saved the eye or not."

Cathy's resolve to "thy will be done" was tougher than she'd anticipated, and the week ahead would present yet another challenge. The night before Wayne's follow-up appointment, he noticed that young Travis was limping badly. His ankle was tender and puffy.

Cathy's day felt like a whirlwind. "I dropped Wayne off at the ophthalmologist's office, then headed with

Travis to see a pediatrician, then on to an orthopedist, who extracted a fluid sample from his swollen ankle." The lab sent test results back in short order, and the news was staggering. Her two-year-old would need emergency surgery on a seriously infected ankle.

In the meantime, Matt, their five-year-old, was waiting to be picked up from the babysitter's house. And Cathy needed to grab some personal belongings so she and Travis could stay overnight at the hospital. Wayne still had patches on his eye, so he couldn't drive. God provided a solution through a neighbor, Betsy, who happened to be at the doctor's office. She would take Wayne home and pick up Matt.

Later on, Cathy sat alone in the waiting room while a surgeon operated on her precious preschooler. She wrestled with worry—and with God. Did she truly want his will above her own, no matter what? Could she entrust even her son's life to him and genuinely mean it? What if the surgery didn't go well? What if it meant losing him?

> WALKING IN TUNE WITH GOD'S WILL BRINGS A PEACE THAT IS BEYOND UNDERSTANDING.

"I had no choice but to lay my small son on the altar of sacrifice, and once again I prayed, 'Thy will be done, Lord.'" Cathy says she whispered that prayer through tears, but meant every word of it from her heart.

After a week in isolation, Travis and his mom were able to return home. "Friends roofed our house," she says with a smile. "Wayne's eye healed. And I learned what it means to truly seek God's will."

Cathy discovered a truth that is learned best in the trenches of life: walking in tune with God's will brings a peace that is beyond understanding. It can strengthen a frightened mother as she waits alone in an emergency room, and it is within the reach of anyone who dares to let go and trust God enough.

Acknowledgments

Abook like this would not be possible if not for those who realized its worth and joined in the effort. My thanks goes to my enthusiastic editor at Standard Publishing, Dale Reeves, who championed the book from day one; to Books & Such agent Wendy Lawton, who possesses the gift of encouragement; and to the following fifty contributors who opened up their hearts and lives so that readers everywhere would be blessed.

1. CINDE LUCAS serves in full-time ministry as an associate evangelist with the United Methodist Church. She is a gifted songwriter, has produced several albums, and travels throughout the U.S. sharing her testimony through word and song with churches, women's groups, and youth groups. For more information visit www.CindeLucas.com.

2. EILEEN ZYGARLICKE, a freelance writer and an English teacher at an alternative high school in North Dakota, loves anything to do with teenagers (given appropriate amounts of coffee, of course).

3. RICK MCNARY grew up a pastor's kid, graduated

from Bethel College in Newton, Kansas, and was a minister for over twenty years. Married, with five children, he currently makes his living as a portrait photographer.

4. CARRIE PAUP lives in Corvallis, Oregon, with her husband and two daughters. For more information about Aicardi Syndrome, visit www.aicardisyndrome.org.

5. JEANELLE RAY's passion for teaching children to read and love books was a natural backdrop for her twenty-five years as an educator. She and her husband live in Abilene, Texas.

6. Freelance writer LEANNE BENFIELD MARTIN lives outside Atlanta, Georgia, with her husband, little girl, and old yellow Lab named Roman. Her work has appeared in many Christian magazines.

7. GAIL HAYES is an international author and speaker who has lived in Japan, Europe, and presently lives in North Carolina. She can be reached through www.daughtersoftheking.org.

8. FLORA REIGADA is a freelance writer whose news stories are published in the *Florida Today* newspaper. Visit her Web site at www.florasbook.com.

9. JULIE KENWARD has been blogging since February 2005 and has had one short story published in the book, *A Light Blazes in the Darkness*, along with her

fellow bloggers from the RevGalBlogPals Web ring. Visit her blog at http://macedwithgrace.squarespace. com.

10. ROGER BRUNER is a former schoolteacher, job counselor/ interviewer, and programmer/analyst who works part-time at a local retail store in Richmond, Virginia. In his spare time he writes faith-based novels and articles for the Faith and Values section at www.richmond.com.

11. LINDA FISCHER (aka BAY ISLE) lives in the state of Washington and has been writing "the heart of God through encouragement and comfort" since 1989.

12. JENNA KING left the corporate world to teach art in elementary schools. A resident of Ohio, she has three middle-grade books in the works.

13. JODY FERGUSON enjoys life with her husband, Gary, outside of Corvallis, Oregon, looking forward to whatever God has in store for them. You may reach her at jody@truenorthdesign.net.

14. JUDY DAVIS retired from the federal government in 2004 and loves to travel. She and her husband, Colin, recently celebrated their fortieth wedding anniversary. They have three grown children and five grandchildren. Judy has been writing since 1985 and has written several books. Her Web site is www.judypdavis.org.

15. Laura Petherbridge is an inspirational author and speaker who has appeared on *Family Life Today* with Dennis Rainey and has written for *Focus on the Family* magazine. She is featured as a divorce recovery expert in the DivorceCare series, and her book *When Your Marriage Dies—Answers to Questions About Separation and Divorce* is published by Cook Communications. She can be contacted at www.LauraPetherbridge.com.

16. Kathy Bruins has written for publications such as *Outreach Magazine, Seek* magazine, and the *Church Herald,* and has published a drama book, *The Acts of Grace.* Visit her Web site at www.kathybruins.com.

17. Laura Farrar is a high school writer in California who helps shy teens discover their voices through writing and speaking. Visit her Web site at www.freewebs.com/laurafarrar.

18. Thomas Smith is an award-winning writer, reporter, TV news producer, playwright, and essayist. In addition to his writing career, Thomas is a professional speaker through his company, LaughLines Ministries. Visit him at www.LaughLinesMinistries.info.

19. Maureen Miller lives in the beautiful mountains of North Carolina with her husband and two boys. She enjoys her friends and family and is ever thankful for the gift of life! She can be reached at adayz4u@yahoo.com.

20. LORI FAIR is a paraeducator who teaches IRC students at the elementary level. She lives in rural Kansas with her husband, daughter, and son and has three grown stepdaughters.

21. REGINA ELCOCK-WINNINGHAM has taught elementary school for more than thirty years, and has been sewing for over forty. She's a youth director and a Sunday school teacher at her church, as well as a loving grandmother who enjoys reading, cooking, and watching the sun rise and set.

22. NANETTE THORSEN-SNIPES has been writing for the Lord for more than twenty years and has published numerous articles, columns, and devotions. She lives in northeast Georgia with her husband and has four children and four grandchildren. She can be contacted at nsnipes@bellsouth.net.

23. VIOLET NESDOLY lives in Surrey, B.C., with her husband, Ernie, and is the mother of two adult children. She has had fiction, nonfiction, and poetry published in a variety of magazines, Sunday school papers, and Web sites. When she isn't writing, she enjoys bird-watching, reading, and singing in her church choir.

24. SHARON BRANI is a mom to two daughters and was an educator for over twenty years. She presently offers healing and hope as a counselor and coach, and can be reached at www.sharonbrani.com.

25. VALERIE WOLFF is a part-time psychotherapist and a columnist for www.christianwomenonline.net. Married for more than thirty years, she lives in Ohio with her husband and two daughters.

26. BECKY BANKS is a freelance writer who lives in Virginia with her two sons and her Yorkiepoo puppy. She's been writing for Fortune 500 companies for at least eighteen years, but is more excited to share her faith journey with Christian readers.

27. SARAH ANNE SUMPOLEC stays busy with her three little girls in Virginia and tries to write in between swim lessons and carpools. She is the author of the YA series *Becoming Beka* and can be found at www.sarahannesumpolec.com.

28. MARION TICKNER has been published in various children's magazines. She also has stories in two anthologies, *Mistletoe Madness and Summer Shorts* (Blooming Tree Press, 2004 and 2006).

29. GLENDA SCHOONMAKER is a motivational speaker, writer, and certified personality trainer. She lives in the desert southwest and has been married to her college sweetheart for almost forty years.

30. CHERRY PEDRICK is the coauthor of seven books, including *The OCD Workbook and The Habit Change Workbook*. She lives in Lacey, Washington, with her husband and four cats.

31. JAMES TEW lives in Kendallville, Indiana, where he is an online editor for the KPC Media Group.

32. GLENDA PALMER is an instructor with the Institute of Children's Literature. She and her husband, Richard, live in the San Diego area.

33. JAN COATES, author of *Set Free*, is a professional writer and speaker. She lives in College Station, Texas, with her husband and two teens. For more information, visit www.jancoates.com.

34. MARY KIRK is a writer, musician, and women's Bible study leader. Mother of five and grandmother of ten, she enjoys reading, writing, and lemon meringue pie.

35. JENNIFER GRAF GRONEBERG lives and writes at the end of a twisty, gravel road with her husband, their three children, two cats, and one dog. She tries to say thank you at least once every day. You can read more about her and her family at www.jennifergrafgroneberg.com.

36. GAY INGRAM writes from the piney woods of east Texas. Her two novels, *'Til Death Do Us Part* and *Troubled Times* are available through www.Amazon.com.

37. LUCY NEELEY ADAMS is the author of *52 Hymn Story Devotions* from Abingdon Press and is the creator of the radio program *The Story Behind the*

Song, which aired for ten years on Christian radio in Nashville, Tennessee. For more information, visit www.52hymns.com.

38. ROY PROCTOR is a freelance writer who produces a daily e-mail column titled "Words for Kingdom Living." He attends Grace Chapel Christian Fellowship in Mandarin, Florida.

39. JANEY DEMEO is founder and director of Orphans First, a ministry to suffering children in the world: www.orphansfirst.org. She is also a pastor's wife, mother of two grown children and author. She and her husband were church planters and missionaries to France for twenty-two years and are now living in Southern California.

40. ARLENE KNICKERBOCKER owns The Write Spot (www.thewritespot.org), which offers writing, editing, teaching, speaking, and desktop publishing services. She has seen hundreds of her devotionals, poems, Sunday school teaching materials, and articles in print and has coauthored one book.

41. A. CHRISTIAN spent his college years as a staff writer for the Republican State Caucus in California. In the twelve years since then, he has served on the foreign mission field, worked in education, and served in the local church. Christian is his pen name.

42. CANDY ARRINGTON's publishing credits include

Today's Christian, Marriage Partnership, Focus on the Family, The Upper Room, and *Writer's Digest.* She is coauthor of *Aftershock: Help, Hope, and Healing in the Wake of Suicide* and is a contributor to numerous anthologies. Contact her at www.CandyArrington.com.

43. Children's and inspirational book writer DONNA J. SHEPHERD looks at everyday life and finds God's fingerprints everywhere. She has written a delightful children's book, *Topsy Turvy Land* (Hidden Pictures Publishing), for young children. Visit Donna on the Web at www.donnashepherd.com.

44. DIANE H. PITTS is a contributing author to *Grace Givers, God Allows U-Turns, Divine Stories of the Yahweh Sisterhood,* and *The Kids' Ark.* She enjoys working as a physical therapist and making a home for her husband and three boys.

45. BARBARA MARSHALL is a CPA and writer who has authored numerous stories and articles for both business and Christian women's publications. She lives in Raleigh, North Carolina, with her husband, Dennis, and can be reached at ofi_barbara@bellsouth.net.

46. KATHERINE BROWN has changed the names in her story, including her own.

47. TWILA SCHOFIELD is an artist who works with New Mission Systems International in Fort Myers,

Florida. She illustrates books and creates visual communication tools for missionaries to use on the field.

48. DENA DYER is a speaker, a singer, the author of *Grace for the Race: Devotionals for Busy Moms* (Barbour), and the coauthor of *The Groovy Chicks' Road Trip* series (Cook). She makes her home in Texas with her husband and two sons. For more information, visit her Web site at www.denadyer.com.

49. HELMER "PETE" PETERSON has ministered to a small community in Iowa for over forty years. He enjoys music, writing, and studying the Bible and eagerly anticipates the Lord's return.

50. CATHY GOEKLER lives on the Oregon coast with her husband and celebrates life through writing, speaking, and photography.

WHEN HAS GOD STEPPED INTO YOUR LIFE?
WRITE ABOUT YOUR EXPERIENCES HERE.

_____

_____

_____

_____

_____

_____

_____

_____

_____

_____

_____

_____

_____

_____

_____

_____

_____

_____

_____

_____

_____

_____

_____

_____

_____

_____

_____

_____

_____

_____

_____

_____

_____

_____

_____

_____

_____

_____

_____

_____

_____